Ancient Manifestation S

"*Ancient Manifestation Secrets* provides a refreshing take on manifestation, combining energy work with cognitive practices to transmute negative emotions and release limiting beliefs. This book is a must-read for anyone serious about going beyond overly simplistic manifestation tools and collaborating with the Universe to manifest their life and purpose."

—GALA DARLING, author of *Magnetic Mindset* and *Radical Self-Love*

"A unique fusion of ancient Greek and Egyptian wisdom with practical manifestation techniques, *Ancient Manifestation Secrets* offers a clear path to discovering and aligning with your higher purpose."

—SHERIANNA BOYLE, life coach, energy healer, and author of *Just Ask Spirit*

"*Ancient Manifestation Secrets* goes against common manifestation teachings by revealing that not all desires are meant to manifest. Instead, George Lizos expertly guides readers in discovering which desires align with their higher purpose and Universal laws, ensuring a more fulfilling and purposeful manifestation journey. This book is a game-changer for those seeking to align their desires with their higher purpose."

—AMY LEIGH MERCREE, medical intuitive, healer, and author of *Aura Alchemy* and *A Little Bit of Chakras*

"George Lizos does an excellent job simplifying the 7 Hermetic laws of the Universe in *The Kybalion* and creating a practical system of working with them to manifest your soul's desires and purpose. The 10-day manifestation challenge makes it even easier to jump in and start working with the laws to create positive changes."

—TAMMY MASTROBERTE, author of *The Universe Is Talking to You*

"In the age of social media, the true essence of things are so often lost behind filters and other curated layers of distortion. George Lizos has harnessed the rare talent of getting to the nut of something, its core. As a beloved acting teacher of mine would say: 'It's the thing under the thing under the thing.' It is in this way that George speaks directly to his readers—as if conversing with a trusted friend or spirit guide—empowering us with the tools needed to work with our own energy field and consciously magnetize our highest desires and purpose."

—JY PRISHKULNIK, actress known for
Monster High: The Movie (2022) and *Just Beyond* (2021)

"George Lizos merges his expertise in energy work with timeless manifestation laws to create an innovative system for manifesting your desires. His approach integrates ancient wisdom, how to work with the universe, and practical techniques, making it simple, accessible, and effective for all spiritual seekers. George has a way of bringing it all further to life and making it enjoyable for the reader/seeker."

—ALI LEVINE, celebrity stylist, certified breathwork coach,
and angel intuitive

"Drawing from ancient Greek and Egyptian teachings, George Lizos debunks the common manifestation myth that negative thoughts manifest your reality and provides powerful techniques for transmuting negative emotions into manifesting energy."

—SUZY ASHWORTH, *Sunday Times* bestselling author of
Infinite Receiving

Ancient MANIFE*S*TATION *Secrets*

Working with the
7 Laws of the Universe to
Manifest Your Life and Purpose

George Lizos

FINDHORN PRESS

Findhorn Press
One Park Street
Rochester, Vermont 05767
www.findhornpress.com

Findhorn Press is a division of Inner Traditions International

Disclaimer
The information in this book is given in good faith and intended for information
only. Neither author nor publisher can be held liable by any person for any loss
or damage whatsoever which may arise from the use of this book or any of the
information therein.

Cataloging-in-Publication data for this title is available from
the Library of Congress

ISBN 979-8-88850-090-3 (print)
ISBN 979-8-88850-091-0 (ebook)

Printed and bound in the United States by Lake Book Manufacturing, LLC.

10 9 8 7 6 5 4 3 2 1

Edited by Jacqui Lewis
Text design and layout by Yasko Takahashi
Illustrations: Yasko Takahashi (p. 78);
ID 143611023 © Artinspiring | Dreamstime.com (p. 89)
This book was typeset in Caslon, FreightSans, Plantin, and Zahrah
with Allura as a display typeface.

To send correspondence to the author of this book, mail a first-class letter to the
author c/o Inner Traditions • Bear & Company, One Park Street, Rochester,
VT 05767, USA and we will forward the communication, or contact the author
directly at https://georgelizos.com.

For my best friend, Sargis

Thank you for being my partner-in-crime
in my spiritual adventures

CONTENTS

PART ONE
THE 7 LAWS OF THE UNIVERSE

PART TWO
LIVING THE LAWS

Step 5: Take Inspired Action

PART THREE
10-DAY MANIFESTATION CHALLENGE

FOREWORD

Having known George Lizos personally and professionally for over six years now, I was honoured and delighted to be asked to write the foreword for his debut manifestation book *Ancient Manifestation Secrets*. Having used George's unique new tools and "take" on the ancient wisdom of the Greek and Egyptians myself, I knew this was going to be an incredible book that would give readers a powerful insight into what's possible with manifestation.

Interest in manifestation and the law of attraction has exploded over the last few years. Although these terms currently seem to be popular buzz words, the principles and laws behind them have existed for thousands of years and of course were brought more to our attention through such incredible books as Napoleon Hill's *Think and Grow Rich* (1937) and Rhonda Byrne's *The Secret* (2006). When I spiritually awakened back in 2016 and learned about the power of manifesting, I knew these classic texts were a fantastic introduction but very quickly I came across my own blocks, inner work, and frustration when my biggest desires were not flowing as quickly as I'd hoped. This challenged me to dive deeper into my own work and manifestation practice and develop practical and energetic tools to make manifesting our desires inevitable.

Over this time of deep-diving into more spiritual and energetic modalities, I found that alignment and our own healing process are vital when it comes to manifesting, and that manifesting is simply a process of alignment. I also learned about the seven energetic laws of the Universe and how these directly impact our manifestations. Suddenly, a lot started to make sense in my own life and in my work as I realized we collectively pigeonhole the law of attraction as the "be all and end all," when really there are other key laws in play every single day. How can we successfully manifest our aligned deepest desires if we are only focusing on one of the seven laws?

Today my manifestation practice looks very different, the *Kybalion*'s seven energetic laws of the Universe play a key role in my work and process and I'm so glad that George is bringing this to the forefront of manifesting with this powerful book. This information will change your life and allow you to see what is truly possible when we work with the laws of the Universe. Manifestation becomes effortless, we learn our cycles, our rhythm, and understand what our manifesting superpowers truly are.

There are some very outdated teachings in the law of attraction sphere that I believe cause more harm than help. This relates to the notion that we attract all things to us—the bad as well as the good. The seven energetic laws of the Universe show us that there is more at play—life is not that black and white and we can work with these energetic laws to begin to understand why we are such powerful creators but also how this is a co-creation process with the Universe.

What I love about *Ancient Manifestation Secrets* is how accessible these incredible tools are to us. I have been working with George's methods, especially the "Plant Your Desire in your Energy Field," "Raise the Vibration of Your Desires," and "Connect with Helpful People," over the last two years. These practices came into my life at the perfect time when I was struggling to break through a metaphorical glass ceiling in my business. I'd had so many incredible results over the years, yet I kept hitting this glass ceiling—George's modalities helped me not only break through this ceiling but smash every goal for that year and more. Now, before I launch anything in my business and especially at the end of the year, these meditations are a non-negotiable for me because of how much they propel me into exactly where I want to be. I am so excited to see what these meditations and teachings do for your life too!

Today marks the start of your energetic manifestation journey and I'm beyond excited that George is sharing these ancient teachings with the world. So often, manifestation books miss the importance of mind, body, spirit when working with manifesting and this is why George's work aligns so perfectly: he's going to get to the nitty-gritty of manifestation with you and help you powerfully attract your deepest desires.

This is the most comprehensive and accessible book on these powerful ancient teachings I have seen to date, designed to assist you with manifesting HUGE up-levelling in your life and with your purpose. Everything is carefully created with you, the reader in mind, and is such a joy to experience. I highly recommend this essential guide to manifesting your wildest dreams with the power of your energy field.

~ **Emma Mumford**, bestselling author of *Positively Wealthy*
and *Hurt, Healing, Healed*

INTRODUCTION

The law of attraction is *not* the most powerful law in the Universe. There, I said it.

Are you triggered? Many people would be. The spiritual culture has become so obsessed with, and almost culty about, the law of attraction, that anyone who attempts to doubt or question it in any way gets instantly cancelled.

Now, don't get me wrong. I don't doubt the existence of the law of attraction and its importance in manifestation. Instead, I'd like to introduce a more nuanced way of understanding and working with it, and one that takes into consideration the other laws of the Universe, too.

As I'm sure you've heard before, the law of attraction has been known and practised since ancient times. Manifestation practices had been hidden from the masses and only practised by spiritual adepts and the elite, in secret groups and mystery schools. The information was passed down from master to student, and only to those who were perceived to be worthy of it.

When the knowledge of the law of attraction reached the masses in the early 2000s, it launched a movement of self-empowerment. Thousands of people stepped into their power and realized that they had the tools to create their own reality. Ancient manifestation practices that had been buried for years were circulated freely, and we were all so excited to try them out in our own lives.

And so, we visualized, scripted, and did positive affirmations. We created manifestation boxes, put up vision boards, and faked it until we made it.

The result? Many people made it, but many people didn't . . .

This created frustration with many, myself included:

What am I doing wrong?

How long do I have to wait for it to work?

Am I not visualizing long enough?

Maybe I'm using the wrong pictures on my vision board.

What if the law of attraction isn't really a thing?

Have you had any of these thoughts before? I know I have. Like you, I jumped on the law of attraction bandwagon as soon as I found out about it. I practised the processes religiously and trusted they were going to transform my life. When they didn't work out the way I expected them to, I got disappointed. But rather than give up on them, I instead decided to do more research.

And so, I got obsessed. I read every manifestation book I could get my hands on and studied with the top teachers in the industry. I attended talks, did workshops, and took part in masterminds. They all pretty much taught the same thing, and it wasn't enough. My questions weren't answered, and my results remained the same.

Yes, I was successfully using the law of attraction to manifest a lot of what I desired, but that wasn't always the case. Also, I wasn't always manifesting the right desires for my highest good, purpose, and potential. I had a hunch that I had been missing something. Something that these books and authors had been missing, or ignoring, as well. So, I decided to go straight to the source: the ancients. Specifically, the ancient Greeks and Egyptians, who famously taught about manifestation.

Well, it turns out the ancients had it down all along. The answers were all there, in their ancient texts and philosophical schools; carefully hidden behind strange analogies, myths, and metaphors. It wasn't easy reading the texts, let alone understanding them, but I persevered (being a native Greek speaker definitely helped).

It turns out, the law of attraction is indeed a very powerful law in the Universe, and one of the main laws to work with for manifestation. That being said, what I'd discovered was that there were other equally powerful laws in the Universe, which worked together with the law of attraction to help us manifest our desires and purpose.

Learning about these laws was the missing piece I needed to master my manifestation game. As soon as I started practising them together, my manifestation practice skyrocketed. As a result of working with all the laws, I manifested three book deals, tripled my business revenue, attracted more students to my online programmes, manifested fulfilling relationships, and so much more.

It felt like letting out a breath I hadn't known I'd been holding in for years! With my newfound knowledge, when a manifestation process didn't work, I knew why. When I couldn't manifest something, I understood the reasons behind it and knew how to shift my focus. Most importantly, these ancient manifestation secrets gave me a broader and more nuanced understanding of manifestation, so that I could focus my energy on the right projects and desires, and the ones that aligned with my highest potential and purpose.

In this book, I'll share with you how you can work with the Universal laws, too, to manifest your desires and purpose. Although you can read about these laws in other books, I explain how they relate to manifestation specifically, and teach you a brand new, five-step process of working with them to master your manifestation game. As part of the process, I introduce never-taught-before energetic manifestation practices and meditations, to help you effortlessly put them into practice.

I'm not going to waste your time with visualization, vision boards, scripting, and all the usual manifestation processes. You already know how to use these, and you've probably had enough of reading about them. These are all powerful processes, and I use them in my manifestation practice daily, too. Instead, I want to empower you with new, energy-focused practices that you can use to both optimize your existing manifestation processes and up-level your practice with new processes.

It's my promise that by the end of this book you'll have gone from feeling confused or frustrated about how to effectively manifest your desires, to having clarity and a step-by-step framework to becoming the master manifestor you were destined to be.

The Kybalion

The primary source behind the spiritual principles I share in this book is *The Kybalion: A Study of the Hermetic Philosophy of Ancient Egypt and Greece*. Originally published in 1908 by the "Three Initiates" (often attributed to the New Thought pioneer William Walker Atkinson), *The Kybalion* summarizes the main principles of hermeticism.

Hermeticism was a philosophical school of thought that emerged in late antiquity, and aimed to communicate, in an easy and practical manner, spiritual wisdom from ancient Greece and Egypt. The two hermetic texts that survived, *Hermetica* and *Corpus Hermeticum*, are essentially a fusion of the Platonic, Pythagorian, and Stoic philosophical schools; also, many of the ideas date back to 2,500-year-old inscriptions in the Egyptian pyramids.[1]

In the ancient times, the hermetic texts were thought to be the direct teachings of Hermes Trismegistus (meaning *thrice great*), a syncretic combination of the Greek god Hermes and the Egyptian god Thoth. Later research has shown that attributing texts to various gods was a popular literary trend in late antiquity, so as to give the texts greater *gravitas*.

Although the current edition of *The Kybalion* is not an ancient text, it demystifies the hermetic writings and philosophy, explains the seven Universal laws in an easy and understandable way, and offers metaphors,

---

[1] Three Initiates. *The Kybalion: Centenary Edition*. New York: TarcherPerigee, 2018.

examples, and practices that help us apply these teachings in the modern world. The term *kybalion* is possibly connected to the cymbal (in Greek, *kymbalo*). The cymbal is an ancient musical instrument that was usually used in rituals to demonstrate the creation of the cosmos in seven sacred sounds, representing the seven Universal laws. The cymbal-player, symbolizing the creative force, is also a popular symbolism in the Pythagorean and Platonic philosophical schools.

How to Read This Book

The book is divided into three parts, to help you both understand and put into practice the seven Universal manifestation laws:

Part One—The 7 Laws of the Universe introduces the manifestation principles of the Universe (including the law of attraction), how they work together, and how to use them practically to manifest your desires and purpose.

Part Two—Living the Laws offers a series of practical processes and meditations that will help you utilize the Universal laws for manifestation. You'll learn my five-step manifestation process, which is based on the seven laws, and use it to advance your attraction power.

Part Three—10-Day Manifestation Challenge guides you through a ten-day practice to manifest a specific desire. Drawing from the laws and practices shared, you'll undertake a daily manifestation challenge geared to help you manifest that specific desire in ten days.

Each section and chapter of the book builds on from the previous one, so it's important that you read the book sequentially. Although a few of the manifestation practices can be done as standalone exercises, many of them are based on the practice of a previous process or the understanding of one or more of the Universal laws.

Since this is a practical book, on many occasions I'll ask you to take pen and paper and write things down. So it'll be beneficial to have a journal dedicated to this journey. Whether it is an electronic or a physical one, keeping all the processes in one place will help you to keep track of your progress and revisit the practices when you need to.

We're in This Together

I'm fully committed to helping you get to the finish line, and I want to be there for you every step of the way. Here's what you can do to help me support you on this journey:

1. **Join my private Facebook Group community, Your Spiritual Toolkit.** This is a safe and supportive community of like-minded lightworkers, who are all on this journey with you. Use this group to ask questions, contribute with your answers, and share your journey through the book. I'm actively involved in the group and I'll be there to cheer you on along the way.

2. **Follow me on Instagram (@georgelizos) and keep me posted on your progress.** Send me DMs and tag me in your posts and stories using the hashtag #AncientManifestationSecrets. I read all of my comments and messages and personally reply to everything.

3. **Download the *Ancient Manifestation Secrets* resources from my website: GeorgeLizos.com/AMS.** These include a checklist of all the processes in the book, which you can tick off as you complete them, along with downloadable guided meditations of many of the processes.

I look forward to hearing from you and supporting you along your manifestation journey. I have every confidence in you, and I can't wait to see you live your highest potential and purpose.

1

THE 7 LAWS
OF THE UNIVERSE

1

THE UNIVERSE

As we venture on this journey of understanding, and ultimately mastering, the ancient art of manifestation, it's important that we go back to the basics and explore the essence and foundation of manifestation.

To do this, we need to ask the questions humans have pondered since the beginning of time:

> *What is God, Source, the Universe?*
>
> *Why does the Universe create?*
>
> *How does creation take place?*

(Throughout the book, I'll use the terms *Source* and *Universe* interchangeably, to refer to what most people think of as *God*. I'll use the capitalized *Universe* when I talk about God, and the lowercase *universe* when I talk about the physical cosmos.)

By understanding the nature of the Universe and the energetic mechanics of manifestation, we also get to understand ourselves and our own capacity to create. As you'll learn in Chapter 3, the law of correspondence states "as above, so below"; therefore, we are physical extensions of the Universe. By knowing the Universe, we get to know ourselves, and our own manifestation abilities.

This won't be a lecture on science. There's a lot we can learn from science, but science can only know the part of the truth that has been proven. When it comes to understanding the bigger picture of things, we have to look beyond science and seek answers in the realm of philosophy. Specifically, we'll look into the beliefs and theories of the ancient Greeks, and how they conceptualized the Universe and manifestation. The ancient Greeks have undoubtedly shaped the development of science, society, spirituality, and life as we know it today. Their ideas have guided our understanding and evolution of spirituality, and many of the beliefs we hold today about the nature of the Universe and manifestation are a rehash of their wisdom.

What Is the Universe?

The Universe has had many names through the years. It's been referred to as God, the Creator, Spirit, Source, Infinite Intelligence, The All, or, as the ancient Greeks referred to it, True Being. In this book I'll refer to it as Source and the Universe, but feel free to think of it in a way that makes most sense to you.

To understand what the Universe is, we first need to accept that it's impossible to do so fully from within our limited human perspective. Although we're physical extensions of the Universe, we're limited by our physicality and can only fully understand its nature when we've transitioned back to it. Instead, what we can do is make educated guesses, which is what humans have done since the dawn of time.

According to ancient Greek spirituality, the Universe has three main characteristics:

1. **The Universe Is Absolute:** The Universe is all that is. There's nothing outside of it, otherwise it wouldn't be The All. This means that the cosmos and anything that's beyond it, in all dimensions, and across time and space, are all part of the Universe. Anything you can think of, or cannot think of because you're not aware of it, is part of the Universe.

2. **The Universe Is Infinite:** Since there's nothing outside of the Universe, there's nothing to define, confine, or limit its boundaries. It's in a constant state of expansion in time and space. Being

infinite and all that is, ever was, and ever will be, the Universe was never created and has always continuously existed. There was no beginning and no ending, for, if there was one, the force that created or ended it would be above it; and that's not possible.

3. **The Universe Is Unchangeable**: The substance of what the Universe is is immutable. It cannot change in its true nature for it is perfect the way it is, and there's nothing to change or improve on. What we perceive as change is simply the constant evolution and expression of the Universe in different forms, states, and energies.

Every single piece of consciousness within the Universe, including ourselves and life as we know it, shares the Universe's absolute, infinite, and unchangeable qualities. If we didn't share these characteristics then we wouldn't be part of the Universe, and that cannot be because there's nothing outside of the Universe.

The Cosmos

The physical universe or the cosmos (not to be confused with the Universe meaning Source), as the ancient Greeks referred to it, is a manifestation, thus an extension of, the Universe (Source), in physical form. In Greek the word *cosmos* means jewel and adornment, as the cosmos is the part of the Universe that has acquired natural order and has attained harmony and beauty. The few remaining parts of the cosmos are referred to as the Tartarus, which derives from the word *tarachē*, which means disorder. These are the parts of the Universe, outside of the cosmos, whose qualities haven't yet been defined.

The cosmos can be thought of as being divided into two levels, the level of it that's eternal and the level that's perishable. The eternal level of the cosmos consists of the invisible substance that makes up its essence: the infinite intelligence and divine life-force energy that flows through and powers all life. At this level, the cosmos maintains the Universe's qualities of being absolute, infinite, and unchangeable. Thus, it was never created and cannot be destroyed. Instead, its internal order arose naturally through a never-ending process of emergence or arising, as each one of its forms emerged through the previous one.

On the other hand, the perishable level of the cosmos consists of the physicality of life, which has a temporal beginning and end. This includes everything we're familiar with in the visible world, including plants, rocks, animals, humans, and the physical universe in general. Although this level of the cosmos is characterized by perishability, nothing actually perishes, but instead transforms and evolves into a different state of being.

Having explored the nature and characteristics of the Universe and the cosmos, what remains in the dark yet is the process through which the Universe created and is constantly creating the cosmos. It's this exact process that captures the heart of manifestation, and therefore it's the process that we also use to manifest our life and purpose.

This process is based on the seven laws of the Universe, as theorized by the hermetics. Each law interconnects with all the others to elaborate the process of manifestation. In the next chapter, we'll explore the law of mentalism that sets the foundation of the creative process.

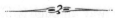

2

THE LAW OF MENTALISM

"The Universe is mental—held in the mind of The All."
—The Kybalion

The law of mentalism states that Source creates mentally. Rather than using physical materials, or reproducing itself, Source creates mental images and intentions that engage the other laws of the Universe to bring that intention into reality.

The Kybalion explains that this is very similar to the way we create mental images in our minds. When we create a mental image, desire, or intention of what we want, we signal to the laws of the Universe to start working towards making that a reality. All laws play a part in the manifestation process, but it all starts with that first mental intention of what we want to create.

The Power of Intention

A key characteristic of this first step of the manifestation process is how Source becomes *involved* or *wrapped up* in its creation, described by *The Kybalion* as the process of involution or outpouring. As Source comes up with a mental intention of a creation, it consistently outpours or extends part of itself into this mental image, and thus, becomes tangled up in its creation.

This is similar to the way through which writers almost become the characters they write about during the creative process. They get so immersed in their characters' minds, feelings, and worlds that they feel as if they *are* the characters while writing about them. When the job is done and the book or script is written, a part of the author still lives within these characters. Yet, the characters aren't the author, and the author isn't the characters. The author simply breathed them to life through a focused process of extending part of themselves into the characters.

Another example of how the mental process of creation works is how an actor almost becomes the character they play for the duration of a play. In their intention to best capture a character's essence, they become wrapped up in the character's thoughts, feelings, and worldview. The actor consciously conjures up a mental image or intention of how they want to perform the character, and then they extend part of their energy and talent to bring that to life. They obsess over their character by thinking like them, feeling like them, and acting like them. Eventually, they bring the character to life in such a visceral way that it seems as if they've become the character.

In truth, although the character contains part of the actor, the character is not the actor. In the same way, the actor is not the character; it's simply a creation.

The key to the mental way through which Source, and therefore, we, manifest, is *sustained mental intention* on our desires. In other words, manifestation occurs when we see ourselves as the authors of our own lives, and go about realizing our desires with the same fervour and intensity with which authors bring their characters to life.

In practical terms, manifestation occurs when we consistently think about, feel about, and visualize having our desires. The operative word here is *consistently*, for this is how we can create a strong enough mental momentum, or outpouring of mental energy, that can drive the manifestation of our desires.

Mental Transmutation

"Mind may be transmuted, from state to state; degree to degree;
condition to condition; pole to pole; vibration to vibration.
True Hermetic transmutation is a mental art."
—The Kybalion

Although the concept of thinking or visualizing our desires into reality sounds simple enough, it's trickier in practice. The majority of manifestation books and trainings out there teach that our thoughts create our reality, but there are still many people who can't seem to make that work. This is partly because there are other factors involved in the manifestation process, which we'll explore in subsequent chapters, but also because we're held back by fears, conditioning, and limiting beliefs that prevent us from sustaining our mental intentions long enough to manifest our desires (more on this in Chapter 8, The Law of Gender).

Obsessively thinking or visualizing about what you want isn't enough to bring it to life. You also have to *feel* what you're thinking and visualizing, and to feel something you need to believe it. For example, if you desire to live a luxurious lifestyle but you currently live pay cheque to pay cheque, it won't be easy for you to think and visualize about your desire and truly believe, and therefore feel, that what you're thinking and visualizing is true. Instead, you'll feel like you're mocking yourself because your emotional state, current experience, and belief system don't support what you're thinking and visualizing.

This is when the art of mental transmutation comes into play. Mental transmutation is about changing or alchemizing your mental, and therefore emotional, state, so that you can believe, and therefore feel, what you're thinking and visualizing. Essentially, mental transmutation is about doing the inner work. It's about identifying and releasing your fears and limiting beliefs, changing your conditioning, and consciously choosing new beliefs and habits that support, and are in alignment with, your desires.

Mental transmutation is the biggest missing piece in the manifestation literature, and the absolute key to mastering manifestation. You can use every single manifestation process out there—affirmations, visualization, scripting, vision boards—but nothing will work until you've aligned your thoughts and visualizations with your beliefs and emotions.

Mental transmutation is the cornerstone of manifestation across the various planes of existence—from the physical realm of animals and humans, to the spiritual realms of spirit guides, deities, and Source. In the next chapter, we'll explore the law of correspondence to understand how this universal harmony can aid your manifestation efforts.

———————⁚———————

3

THE LAW OF CORRESPONDENCE

"As above, so below; as below, so above."
—The Kybalion

The law of correspondence states that the laws of the Universe manifest across all planes of existence. As a result, there is correspondence, harmony, and agreement between the different planes within Source and the cosmos. There's a lot that we can learn about manifestation through this understanding, so let's first consider the various planes of existence.

Source expresses primarily through three main planes of existence:

1. **The Physical Plane:** This primarily consists of physical matter, including solids, liquids, and gases; ether, which is the medium that facilitates the transmission of information between matter and energy; and energy, which includes heat, light, magnetism, electricity, and life-force, as well as forms of energy not yet acknowledged by science and which the human mind can't yet fully comprehend.

2. **The Mental Plane:** This is subdivided into the mineral, plant, elemental, animal, and human minds. The mineral, plant and elemental minds correspond to the states and conditions of the elemental kingdoms, and include the fairies, gnomes, mermaids, and other types of elementals. The animal mind relates to the states and conditions of the world's animals, and the plane of the human mind comprises the states and conditions of humans.

3. **The Spiritual Plane**: The final plane of existence consists of the plethora of spiritual beings, such as gods and goddesses, adepts and Ascended Masters, angels, archangels, and other types of spirit guides.

What's important to understand about these three main planes of existence is that there isn't a clear-cut distinction or separation between them. Although we place them into categories so we can better understand them, in truth there's a fluid relationship between the various planes.

Additionally, the planes of existence aren't places, states, or conditions, although they behave as such in many ways. Instead, they correspond to different levels of vibrational frequency. The lower physical planes have a lower and denser vibrational frequency, and as you move up to the higher spiritual planes the frequency increases.

Interacting with the Other Planes

Since there's correspondence and fluidity between the various planes of existence, we can lower or raise our vibration to interact with them. On a human level, we can raise or lower our vibrational frequency by shifting our emotions. At a soul level we can do so through our soul's journey of ascension; by learning and evolving spiritually from lifetime to lifetime.

From a manifestation standpoint, there's a lot we can achieve by attaining vibrational harmony with the various planes of existence. The elementals, who are the spirits and consciousness of nature, are master manifestors. Many of them have been here since the creation of our planet, and have been responsible for both its sustenance and evolution. If there's anything I learned in my geography degree, it's that our planet doesn't really need saving; it's us that need to be saved. Planet Earth has existed for 4.5 billion years while humans have been on the planet for only 200,000 years, which is a blink of an eye in the Earth's timeline.

Throughout its existence, our planet has seen many forms of life and has experienced all kinds of destructions. Yet, every single time it's come out a winner. The Earth has powerful processes, powered by the elementals, to flush out impurities and maintain her balance. When we attune our vibrational frequency to partner with the elementals, we're able to learn and benefit from their manifestation and recalibration secrets.

At the spiritual planes of existence, we can also work with various spirit guides to support our manifestation efforts. The gods and goddesses of the ancient Greeks, and other earth-based traditions, are extensions and expressions of the various aspects, functions, and laws of the Universe. Their purpose is intrinsically tied in with the establishment and maintenance of order, across all planes of existence. Aside from the gods who oversee the smooth functioning of the cosmos, other spiritual beings such as the angels, archangels, unicorns, and Ascended Masters also take interest in the functioning of the cosmos, and generously offer their help and influence to those who ask for and are ready to receive it.

Although the beings at the spiritual plane share the same manifestation laws as us, they have already mastered, and can easily and expertly use them to manifest their desires. When we consciously raise our vibration to communicate and ask for their help, they will impart to us their manifestation secrets, which we can use to develop our abilities further.

Spiritual Ascension and Manifestation

The second way we can raise our vibration to connect with, and benefit from, the spiritual plane's manifestation expertise is via our soul's journey of ascension. We live hundreds, if not thousands of lifetimes, during which we work our way up the planes of existence, from the physical, to the mental, and finally to the spiritual one. The degree to which we ascend up the ascension scale depends on our capacity to fulfil our life purpose and learn the lessons we're meant to learn in each lifetime.

Here's how this works:

All lightworkers[2] have four main purposes. These are the collective lightworker purpose, soul realm purpose, soul purpose, and life purpose. The collective lightworker purpose is our shared purpose of ascending the vibration of the planet and helping create a kinder, more equal, loving, and peaceful world. The soul realm purpose is the collective purpose of our soul realm. Soul realms are groups of souls that share a common mission and characteristics, such as starseeds and wise ones. The individual soul purpose is a purpose that draws from our realm's purpose, and it involves a large-scale project to be fulfilled over a series of lifetimes. Finally, the life purpose is a step towards fulfilling our soul purpose, and therefore our mission to fulfil in our current lifetime.

As we focus on finding and following our life purpose in the current lifetime, we simultaneously follow our soul, soul realm, and collective lightworker purposes. By following and fulfilling our life and soul purposes, we move up the ascension scale, and eventually cross over the threshold of the human mental plane to the spiritual plane, joining forces with the spiritual beings and masters there. The higher up we are on the ascension scale, the more we understand and master the manifestation process.

That being said, it's important to understand that although, as we move up the ascension scale, we become better manifestors, the type and quality of our desires change. As I mentioned earlier, the gods, goddesses, angels, and other spiritual beings in the higher spiritual planes are interested in maintaining the order in the cosmos. Therefore, their desires have evolved beyond living a comfortable physical life (since they're no longer physical) to upholding, improving, and evolving the state and internal functioning of the cosmos.

---

[2] Lightworkers are old, mature souls, who incarnate on the planet for the purpose of raising the vibration of the world. Essentially, they're here to help make the world a better place.

Although it'll take many more lifetimes until we've transitioned to the spiritual plane of existence, we can still benefit from this enlightened perspective of manifestation through consciously raising our vibration to the spiritual plane's frequency. As we consciously, through our spiritual practice, raise our vibration and make contact with the beings in the spiritual plane, we not only receive their help, but also become attuned to their collective spiritual mind. This allows us to receive their guidance more easily, follow our life purpose more effectively, and ultimately speed up our soul's journey of ascension.

In the next chapter, we will dive into what is probably the most popular Universal law, and the most practical one when it comes to mastering manifestation and speeding up our soul's journey of ascension. This is none other than the law of vibration, which is more commonly known as the law of attraction.

4

THE LAW OF VIBRATION

"Nothing rests; everything moves; everything vibrates."
—The Kybalion

The law of vibration states that everything in the Universe and in the cosmos vibrates, and the only difference between one manifestation and another is the varying frequency of vibration. In other words, when you zoom into every physical piece of consciousness in the Universe, all you'll find is different rates and modes of vibration. Quantum physics has already proven this by explaining that atoms behave as waves, and therefore as vibration.

Aside from the physical, visible world, the invisible world of thoughts, emotions, and spirit, are also vibration. *The Kybalion* tells us that there's a scale of vibration, with the grossest form of matter on one end having the lowest vibrational frequency, and Spirit on the other end with the highest vibrational frequency. In between the two poles, there are millions upon millions of different frequencies of vibration, representing the totality of physical and non-physical manifestations in the Universe.

How Attraction Works

Since everything is made up of the same kind of vibrating substance, the entire Universe can be seen as a massive vibrational web of energy, with the various nodes within the web corresponding to the various manifestations in the Universe. To manifest anything, one needs to consciously access that vibrational web and attune to the frequency of their chosen desire.

This is achieved through the process of mental transmutation, as explained in Chapter 2. As humans, our way of changing our vibrational frequency to match the vibration of a desire has to do with transmuting our beliefs, thoughts, and emotions. Our beliefs create thoughts,[3] and our thoughts create emotions, which in turn affect our vibrational frequency. Mental transmutation has to do with using processes to consciously shift our beliefs, thoughts, and emotions to different ones, for the purpose of manifesting our desires and purpose.

To better understand how this works, consider the emotional guidance scale developed by the non-physical group of consciousness known as Abraham, channelled by Esther Hicks:[4]

1. Joy/Appreciation/Empowerment/Freedom/Love
2. Passion
3. Enthusiasm/Eagerness/Happiness
4. Positive Expectation/Belief
5. Optimism
6. Hopefulness
7. Contentment
8. Boredom
9. Pessimism
10. Frustration/Irritation/Impatience
11. Overwhelment (feeling overwhelmed)
12. Disappointment
13. Doubt
14. Worry
15. Blame
16. Discouragement
17. Anger
18. Revenge

19. Hatred/Rage
20. Jealousy
21. Insecurity/Guilt/Unworthiness
22. Fear/Grief/Desperation/Despair/Powerlessness

This emotional scale shows the 22 main emotions, and therefore vibrational frequencies, that we usually experience as humans. This is different from the scale of vibration described earlier, which consists of the totality of vibrations in the entire Universe. The emotional guidance scale is simply a framework of human emotions, which exist within our human mental (which is also emotional) plane of existence.

The emotions at the top of the scale, such as joy, appreciation, empowerment, freedom, and love, have the highest vibrational frequency, while the emotions at the bottom of the scale, such as fear, grief, despair, and powerlessness, have the lowest vibrational frequency.

To manifest anything, you have to match your vibrational frequency to the vibrational frequency of that which you desire. The easiest way to achieve this is to match your vibrational frequency to the vibrational frequency of *already having* what you desire. Essentially, you need to identify what having your chosen desire feels like, and nurture that emotion consistently. The key word is *consistently*, as it's our dominant vibrational frequency that the Universe responds to, rather than our fleeting, moment-to-moment emotional state.

---

[3] While beliefs create thoughts, thoughts also create beliefs. The two are not mutually exclusive. As Abraham-Hicks rightfully teach, "a belief is just a thought we keep thinking."

[4] Esther and Jerry Hicks wrote some of the most influential books about manifestation and the law of attraction, the most popular one being *Ask and It Is Given* (Hay House, 2004). While the books are written by Esther Hicks, she did so while channelling a group of consciousness who call themselves Abraham. Therefore, the work is often attributed to Abraham-Hicks, which explains this connection.

Embodying the Vibration of Source

An alternative way of manifesting your desires is by raising your vibrational frequency to the frequency of Source. Since Spirit is at the top of the Universal vibrational scale, to vibrate at the frequency of Source we have to raise our vibrational frequency to the highest one we can reach from within our limited human state. This is the frequency right at the top of the emotional guidance scale, the frequency and emotions of joy, appreciation, empowerment, freedom, and love.

In spiritual truth, all your desires, including the fulfilment of your life purpose, are already manifested vibrationally and are ready for you to receive. They're stored in your very own vibrational safe, waiting for you to find the secret pin and let them physically manifest in your life. The secret pin to your vibrational safe is none other than the frequency of Source. This is because Source's frequency is so high that when you vibrate there consistently it'll take over your entire being, and raise your vibration in relation to all your desires.

The added benefit of consistently embodying the vibration of Source as your go-to manifestation process is that you don't have to worry about or micromanage your vibrational state in relation to your many desires. Your work is to stay in alignment with Source, and let that pure, high-vibrational connection saturate your entire being and manifest your desires at the perfect time. Simultaneously, because by raising your vibration to the frequency of Source you access the spiritual plane of existence, you also have your spirit guides and the entire Universe working with you, helping to bring your desires and purpose to life.

In the next chapter, we will delve into the law of polarity. This principle will provide you with valuable insights into navigating the emotional guidance scale as you work toward embodying the vibrational frequency of your desires.

5

THE LAW OF POLARITY

"Everything is dual; everything has poles; everything has its pair of opposites; like and unlike are the same; opposites are identical in nature, but different in degrees; extremes meet; all truths are but half-truths; all paradoxes may be reconciled."

—The Kybalion

The law of polarity is directly connected to the law of vibration, and states that all manifestations, whether physical or immaterial, have two vibrational poles, with many degrees of vibration between them. Love and fear, abundance and poverty, good and evil, Spirit and matter, are all seemingly opposing manifestations that are really two sides of the same coin.

In between each of these poles exist a myriad of vibrational degrees. The emotional guidance scale discussed in the previous chapter is an accurate representation of the polarity between love and fear. Although the two emotions feel contrasting to one another, they really both exist on the same pole, with many different emotions (therefore, vibrational frequencies) between them.

Essentially, the law of polarity teaches that, wherever we are on our specific desire's vibrational scale, we have the opportunity to change our vibrational frequency and match a different, desired frequency—as long as it's on the same scale. For example, if you experience fear, you have access to love; if you experience poverty, you have access to abundance; if you experience loneliness, you have access to companionship.

Isn't this liberating to know? Isn't it liberating to know that simply by experiencing a specific negative state, whether it is an emotion or a state of life, you're on the same vibrational scale as its improvement? Simply, whatever stage you are at on your journey to manifesting your desires and purpose, you already have vibrational access to their manifestation, just by being on the desires' scales.

The Poles Are Limitless

What's important to understand about the law of polarity is that the various pairs of poles are liminal in nature, and thus can never truly be defined as fixed states. In other words, there's no limit to how much love or hate one can experience, and there's no limit to how poor or abundant one can be. Each side of the coin is limitless in nature, and we only define the two opposites so that we can better understand the concept.

This means that, when it comes to your desires, there's no limit to how successful you can be. There's no limit to the happiness you can experience, the fulfilling family life you can have, the love you can feel towards your partner, the impact you can make on your purpose, and the money you can attract in your life. The law of polarity liberates our self-imposed limits of what's possible, giving us the opportunity to raise our standards and give ourselves permission to live a fuller life.

You Have Unlimited Universal Support

Since the poles of everything are limitless in nature, that means that our capacity to raise our vibration to communicate with the spiritual plane of existence is also limitless. We often limit our capacity to access and receive guidance from Source—whether this is through connecting with elementals, angels, spirit guides, or gods and goddesses—thinking that there's a limit as to who we can connect with, the kind of relationship we can have with Spirit, and the degree to which we can be supported.

In truth, there's no limit! There's no limit to how much the Universe can support you on your manifestation journey. There's no limit to how much your spirit guides can shower you with their guidance. There's no limit to your capacity to access and receive that support, as long as you're willing to do so, and take forward action towards it.

Using the Law of Polarity

Effectively using the law of polarity in your manifestation efforts involves awareness coupled with mental transmutation. To begin with, in order to move up the vibrational scale of the state you're in you need to first become aware of that state. From this perspective, awareness involves becoming conscious of, and making a note of, the emotional state you're in on the vibrational scale of your chosen desire.

For example, if your desire involves manifesting a partner, you need to become aware of your current emotional state in relation to that. It's not enough to note that you're single and have that be your vibrational degree on the scale. As mentioned previously, our vibrational frequency in relation to any desire is directly correlated to our emotions. Therefore, the most accurate way of figuring out our current stage on any scale is by considering our current *dominant* emotional state in relation to each desire. For example, being single and heartbroken is different from being single and at peace with it. The two states have a completely different vibrational frequency and are on a different point on your desire's scale.

Once you've identified your current point on your desire's vibrational state, the next step is to use the various mental transmutation processes in Part Two of the book to move up the scale until you match the frequency of your desire.

In the next chapter, you'll learn how the law of polarity interacts with the laws of rhythm and vibration, and how you can leverage this interaction to master mental transmutation. These triad of laws are the most practical of the seven laws when it comes to manifestation.

6

THE LAW OF RHYTHM

"Everything flows out and in; everything has its tides; all things rise and fall; the pendulum swing manifests in everything; the measure of the swing to the right, is the measure of the swing to the left; rhythm compensates."

—The Kybalion

The law of rhythm states that there's a pendulum-like movement between the two poles of all manifestations on the physical, mental, and spiritual planes. There's a cyclical nature in everything; a flow and inflow, rise and fall, growth and decay. Nature flourishes during the spring and summer months and dies out during autumn and winter; nations rise and fall; the economy goes from a boom to a recession. Similarly, human emotions oscillate from positive emotions such as joy and love to negative emotions such as fear and depression.

It is primarily in the field of human emotions that the law of rhythm comes into play when it comes to manifesting our desires. Understanding how it works can help us amplify it when it's swinging in our favour, and rise above it when it isn't.

Since, as per the law of polarity, the two poles of any manifestation are liminal, limitless, and undefined in nature, the rhythm of the pendulum from one pole to the other is equally so. In other words, the pendulum almost never swings to the extremes of each pole. Instead, each manifestation experiences variability in both the timing and the extent of the swings.

The Law of Compensation

The variability of rhythm from pole to pole depends on many factors, one of which is determined by the law of compensation.

When it comes to human emotions, states, and conditions, the swing of the pendulum depends on our past experiences. The law of compensation states that "the capacity of pain and pleasure in each individual is balanced." Therefore, the worse it is, the better it can get. The more grief, pain, poverty, or illness one can experience, the more happiness, pleasure, abundance, and health one can experience too. Whatever extent of an emotional state or condition you may be at, you automatically have access to, and can experience, its exact opposite.

This doesn't mean that for you to manifest the love, happiness, and abundance that you seek you first need to experience their opposite in this lifetime. The laws of rhythm and compensation see beyond your current incarnation and perceive the whole, eternal, soul You, who has had hundreds, if not thousands, of past lives. Chances are you *have* experienced the downward swing of the pendulum in many different emotional states and conditions at some point in your soul's journey. Therefore, you have an opportunity in the present lifetime to experience the upward swing of things.

The Law of Neutralization

The Hermetics believed that although you can't skip, avoid, or break the laws of the Universe, you can use other laws to overcome them. This isn't about breaking one law by using another, but rather understanding how laws work with each other and using this information to work with the laws in a more complex way.

The law of neutralization is such a law; one which can help us neutralize the backward swing of the pendulum by polarizing ourselves towards the positive pole.

The Kybalion explains that, by consciously and consistently raising our vibration to vibrate at the higher end of the pole, we soften our experience of the backward swing. Rather than escaping, avoiding, or being in denial of the backward swing, we instead raise our consciousness to a higher frequency that can better understand and handle the negativity of the backward swing. Essentially, by mastering our capacity to nurture and maintain a high vibrational frequency, we become more resilient and have a bird's-eye view of situations, and thus aren't as negatively affected by them.

As we commit to the daily practice of raising our vibration, we eventually raise our *overall* vibrational frequency, and thus polarize to the positive swings of all our poles. This way, we still experience the backward swings of our various emotional states and conditions, but the resulting impact on our overall vibration and quality of life is reduced. As a result, our vibration remains high most of the time, upholding our manifestation effort and power.

Amplifying the Upward Swing

Neutralizing the backward swing of the pendulum can help us pacify negative emotions and conditions and keep our vibration high. Conversely, amplifying and extending the upward swing of the pendulum can help us boost our manifestation abilities.

You know the pendulum is swinging upwards when you're in the flow. People show up to support you, opportunities come your way plentifully, and life unfolds easily and effortlessly. You wake up in the morning feeling excited for the day ahead and everything you set out to do unfolds without effort or struggle. Life feels good, you feel good, the people around you feel good, and you're living your best life.

What most people do when the pendulum swings upwards in any area of their lives is just sit back and enjoy the ride. Although there's nothing wrong with doing so, I'd much rather see you ride that upward swing harder! In other words, since there's no limit to how high the pendulum can swing, why not try to extend it? Why just feel happy when you're given the opportunity to feel ecstatic? Why just be content in your relationship when you're able to make it fun and exciting? Why settle for a comfortable lifestyle when you know you can experience luxury?

Amplifying the upward swing isn't about being greedy, but about raising your standards to match the Universe's standards for you. Your higher self already knows you're supposed to live an extraordinary life. Extending the upward swing of the pendulum is about stepping into that truth and living life from your higher self's perspective.

Although the triad of laws of vibration, polarity, and rhythm allow us to take control of our vibrational frequency and play an active role in manifesting our desires, there are other factors involved in manifestation. In the next chapter, you'll learn about these factors and understand how the law of cause and effect orchestrates them in the manifestation process.

7

THE LAW OF CAUSE AND EFFECT

"Nothing happens by chance; chance is merely a term indicating cause existing but not recognized or perceived ... there can be no such agent as 'chance', in the sense of something outside of Law—something outside cause and effect."
—The Kybalion

The law of cause and effect teaches that nothing happens by chance. Instead, there's a logical cause behind every effect. What we call chance or luck is simply causes that we cannot perceive or understand. From this perspective, our manifestations are the results of a long string of causes and effects. Simultaneously, they're also the causes of more effects, and therefore new manifestations.

What *The Kybalion* makes clear about manifestation is that there's no such thing as creating something, but rather a natural and never-ending unfolding of a series of cause-and-effect events. To create something would imply that you start from zero; but nothing can truly start from zero, as there are always multiple preceding events leading to the manifestation of a desire.

To consciously manifest something, we need to be cooperative components of the causation process. We first need to be the creation of causes, through our thoughts/intentions, our emotions/vibrations, and our actions. Secondly, we need to be cooperative components of the causes that are already in place, and that we may not yet be aware of.

The majority of the literature on manifestation stresses the importance of the law of attraction, thus the law of vibration, in manifesting our desires and purpose. As a result, we've considered our thoughts and emotions to be our main causes for manifestation. Although our thoughts and emotions are indeed our primary tools, through which we can be causes in the manifestation of our desires, there are more factors involved.

Is the Law of Attraction the Most Powerful Law in the Universe?

Popular spiritual culture teaches that the law of attraction/vibration is the most powerful law in the Universe. I previously held this belief myself, but my subsequent research, experience, and understanding of Universal laws has taught me otherwise. I believe that the law of attraction is certainly a powerful law in the Universe; but there are also many other powerful laws, and therefore causes, that the law of attraction has to work with.

In other words, the law of attraction isn't more powerful than the law of gravity. However much you raise your vibration or change your beliefs to believe you can fly, you really can't. The law of gravity won't let you because, guess what—in this respect, it's more powerful than the law of attraction. The same is true for most of our physical characteristics. We may try all we want to change our height, hair colour, or facial features just with the power of our minds, but that goes against the laws of biology, and is therefore impossible.

How Miracles Take Place

But, what about miracles? What about the hundreds of stories of using the power of the mind to heal seemingly incurable diseases? Aren't these proof of the law of attraction surpassing other laws to create change? The answer is yes, and no.

In every single *real* story of a "miraculous" healing there has been a chain of cause-and-effect events leading up to it. The reason we may perceive them as miracles is because we're not always aware of the complex series of causes behind them. One of these causes may have been utilizing the law of attraction using positive thoughts and emotions to contribute to a positive outcome; but there will also have been other causes involved.

As discussed in the previous chapter, the laws of the Universe work together in complex and cooperative ways, so that you can at times use one law to curb the impact of the other. This doesn't mean that you beat one law with another, but rather that you can work with the laws in a more nuanced way.

The ancients understood miracles in a very different way than we do today. Our modern perception of a miracle is one of supernatural events— something that goes above the laws of the Universe. But the existence of an event that goes above or against the laws of the Universe would imply that there's a power above the Universe, which, as I explained earlier, is impossible. Conversely, the ancient Greeks believed that miracles are natural events in a chain of causes and effects that are in accordance with the laws of the Universe. From this perspective, miracles do take place, but the miracles are merely manifestations of people understanding and utilizing the laws of the Universe to allow an improved state of being.

Unknown and Little-Known Causes

As mentioned earlier, there are many causes beyond the law of attraction that contribute to the manifestation process, many of which are often disregarded by popular spirituality. This results in frustration when our manifestation processes don't work, making us feel inadequate and wonder what it is we're doing wrong. As a result, we keep on buying more books and courses, learning the same limited perspectives on manifestation, which keep us stuck in the cycle.

The only way to break free is by educating ourselves about the lesser-known causes that contribute to the manifestation process. The seven Universal laws in this book are the main causes, but there are more.

Here's a list of the most prevalent little-known factors that contribute to manifestation also:

1. **Soul Contracts:** Soul contracts are promises and plans we made before our present incarnation about the lessons we wanted to learn in the course of our lifetime. Many soul contracts involve our relationships with people, and the roles we decided to play in each other's lives. Other soul contracts have to do with certain virtues, skills, talents, and qualities we wanted to develop, as well as the various achievements we wished to accomplish. Soul contracts are so called because they're decided on a soul level, and they aim at helping our soul ascend on its spiritual journey of evolution to enlightenment.

   The reason certain manifestations sometimes don't manifest is because they may not be in accordance with one or more of our soul contracts. Although our vibration may be creating a cause for the desired effect, there may be a bigger, stronger cause behind it already in place that originated before our incarnation.

2. **Fate:** We often approach the subject of free will versus determinism in an absolute, black-and-white manner. Some people believe that everything is fated to happen and there's nothing we can do about it, while others take the approach that we are the sole determinants of our future. I believe the answer is more balanced.

   The ancient Greeks personified fate into three goddesses known as the Three Fates. The first is Lachesis, who's said to visit each newborn baby on their first night and plan the main, large-scale events in the baby's life. Although she determines the occurrence of these events, she doesn't determine their outcome; this depends on the person's free will.

The second goddess is Clotho, who's responsible for weaving these main events into manifestation at the right time in the person's life.

Lastly, Atropos determines when the person's life will eventually end, thus the person's death.

Essentially, this perspective on fate is very much in alignment with our soul contracts. Certain events and circumstances are set in stone and are fated to happen, but, as they do, we always have free will to change them if we so wish to. Consequently, for a desire to manifest it has to be in alignment with these fated, soul agreements.

3. **Our Four Purposes**: Remember the four purposes of lightworkers that I shared in Chapter 3? Our first purpose is the collective lightworker purpose that has to do with raising the overall vibration of the world. The second purpose is the soul realm purpose, which involves a larger-scale collective purpose shared among people within our soul realm, which is our soul's origin. Our soul purpose draws from the soul realm purpose and is a large-scale mission fulfilled over a series of lifetimes, whereas our life purpose is a step towards fulfilling our soul purpose, and is therefore very specific to our unique set of skills, talents, and abilities.

For a desire to easily manifest in our life it has to be in alignment with our four purposes, primarily the life and soul purposes. If it isn't, although we can still manifest that desire it'll be harder to do so, as it won't be in alignment with what we came here to be and do. Additionally, manifesting a desire that isn't in alignment with our life and soul purpose may set us back in the fulfilment of our purpose.

4. **Collective Manifestation:** Although what we manifest in our lives is primarily an outcome of our personal, conscious, or unconscious understanding and use of Universal laws, there's also a degree of collective manifestation taking place. Since we live in a shared and therefore interconnected world, we're not only influenced by those around us but we also manifest together.

   From our souls' collective perspective, before we chose to partake in the human experiment on planet Earth we set up collective contracts and agreements as to what we wanted to achieve and experience together. From a human perspective, each thought we think and emotion we feel contributes to humanity's collective vibrational frequency, which goes on to shape, to a great degree, our collective reality. The COVID-19 pandemic, and other large-scale events such as wars, financial depressions, and technological advancements, are all prime examples of such collective manifestations.

Manifestation Is Universal Collaboration

With these factors in mind, manifestation isn't just about our personal, human point of attraction. Instead, it's a collaborative process that involves our whole, multidimensional self along with the entire human and Universal consciousness. To manifest anything, our desires need to be in alignment with not just our mental and emotional outlook, but also the aforementioned factors and Universal laws.

Frankly, what I've learned in my journey to mastering manifestation, and what I hope you can now begin to understand, too, is that the Universe is not our bitch! Manifesting our desires and purpose isn't about willing the Universe to do our bidding. It's about understanding our purpose, soul contracts, and collective manifestation, and partnering with the laws of the Universe to co-create the desires that will allow us to both fulfil our purpose and also fulfil our collective purpose of raising the vibration of the world.

Although taking so many factors into consideration may make manifestation seem like a complicated task, it really is simpler than it seems. Your soul is already connected with, and aware of, all the various factors and Universal laws contributing to manifestation. Your soul knows your life purpose and soul's journey of ascension, and therefore knows the exact desires that you need to manifest to follow that. Consequently, any desire that comes out of a state of alignment with your soul is already in accordance with the aforementioned factors, and can easily manifest into your life.

To master manifestation, then, you have to nurture and sustain a connection with your soul, so you can receive the desires that are already in accordance with the multiple factors involved in manifestation, as well as the guidance needed to bring them to life.

In the next chapter, you'll learn how the law of gender can help you receive desires that are already aligned with your soul and highest good, as well as guide you in taking balanced action in your manifestation efforts.

8

THE LAW OF GENDER

"Gender is in everything; everything has its masculine and feminine principles; gender manifests on all planes."
—The Kybalion

The word "gender" is derived from Latin and it means "to generate, create, and produce." Our modern understanding of the word gender to refer to biological sex (male/female/intersex[5]), or social gender (man/woman/genderqueer), is simply a way through which gender expresses on the physical and social planes. From a spiritual and energetic perspective, the office of gender has to do with the process of creation.

The Kybalion teaches that gender is at the basis of the manifestation process, in that the masculine and feminine energies are both intrinsically involved in the creation of things. Simultaneously, everything in the world is made of, and balanced in, both energies.

A prime example of how masculine and feminine energies drive the manifestation process is the way through which atoms are formed. Essentially, atoms come together when a positive ion (masculine energy) exerts

---

[5] "Intersex" refers to a variety of conditions in which an individual's reproductive or sexual anatomy doesn't fit the typical definitions of female or male. This can involve variations in chromosomes, hormones, or physical structures. Intersex might be apparent at birth due to visible differences in genitalia, or it might be discovered later in life, such as during puberty or through genetic testing. Not all intersex conditions are visibly apparent. Sometimes, the terms Differences in Sex Development (DSD), Disorders of Sex Development, Variations in Sex Characteristics (VSC), or Diverse Sex Development are used.

influence on a negative ion (feminine energy), allowing for an atom to be created. Since atoms are the physical make-up of everything on the physical plane, and since by the law of correspondence the same laws govern all planes of existence, then all creation, whether it's on the physical, mental, or spiritual plane, is created by the interplay of, and is balanced in, masculine and feminine energy.

The Gendered Process of Creation

Masculine and feminine energies play distinctive roles in the manifestation process. Masculine energy is the one that directs and expresses energy, thus getting the creative process started and seeing things to completion. It creates a framework and a plan of action, and directs the action-taking required for things to manifest. Masculine energy is like a project manager, choosing the right team and materials, handing out responsibilities, and orchestrating the manifestation process.

On the other hand, feminine energy receives instructions, makes sense of them, creates space for manifestation, and does the generating work of bringing the manifestations to life. Simply put, masculine energy directs the energy of creation and feminine energy is the womb that births them into the world.

The way through which masculine and feminine energy manifests within us in the creation process has to do with our capacity to receive intuitive guidance on the way to manifesting our desires (feminine energy), and using this guidance to plan and take forward action (masculine energy). To successfully manifest anything, we have to be balanced in both energies.

Balancing Our Masculine and Feminine Energies

Most people are imbalanced in their masculine and feminine energies, which prevents them from successfully following their purpose and manifesting their desires.

To begin with, the patriarchal world we live in values masculine energy more than feminine energy. As a result, we've been conditioned to hustle, struggle, and take mindless action towards our purpose without consulting with our intuition first. Rather than letting our feminine energy inform our action-taking, we instead abuse and over-depend on our masculine energy, which creates an imbalance.

If we don't overuse our masculine energy, we do so with our feminine energy. This is true for many people who have either burned out at an earlier stage in their life, or have experienced abuse by patriarchal forces in this or their past lifetimes. Afraid to use their masculine energy in case they abuse it, or be abused by it, they instead find comfort in receiving intuitive ideas about their purpose but never take action towards them.

Because our world has been imbalanced in masculine and feminine energy for thousands of years, we often don't know how to go about finding balance. We've lived out of balance for such a long time that we're conditioned to abuse either our masculine or feminine energy.

The easiest way I've found of balancing the two energies within us is by consciously and consistently connecting and realigning ourselves with our inner being, and therefore Source, through our spiritual practice. Source is already perfectly balanced in masculine and feminine energy, and so by regaining our connection to it we automatically find balance too.

Mental Gender

When it comes to using the law of gender consciously for manifestation, we also need to understand how the principle of gender manifests not just on the physical level but also on the mental one, as this is where manifestation begins.

The Kybalion distinguishes between masculine and feminine energy on the mental plane by explaining the difference between the two main identity pronouns we use to understand ourselves, the "I" and the "me."

When we think of "me," we are usually referring to our physical and personality characteristics and desires. We think of the way our body looks, our feelings, beliefs, hobbies, likes and dislikes, and all the ways through which we define our human incarnation. The "me" is the already manifested version of ourselves, and thus it's more aligned with our feminine energy.

On the other hand, the "I" that is us is rooted in our consciousness and is more aligned with our will to create, rather than what already is created. The "I" comes up with ideas, desires, and intentions and projects them onto the "me," so that they can be manifested. As a result, the "I" is our masculine mental energy, the one that starts, directs, and operates the creation process.

In practical terms, on the mental plane the masculine energy within us comes up with an intention and desire to manifest something and our feminine energy conducts the work of nurturing thoughts and emotions, which will allow that desire to grow momentum and eventually manifest in our lives.

Where Do Your Desires Come From?

A question to ask yourself is, where is your "I" getting its intentions and desires from? Are your desires an extension of your authentic self and purpose, or are they influenced by other people's desires for, and expectations of, you?

Although we're born knowing our life purpose and have a direct connection to Source, who can guide us in following it, as we grow up we're inevitably indoctrinated and conditioned by our family, the school system, and society at large. At first, we rebel, resist, and hold on to our authenticity. Eventually, they break us and we end up buying into their cookie-cutter formula for being and living. We forget our life purpose, lose our connection to Source, and end up thinking other people's thoughts, feeling other people's emotions, and behaving in ways that aren't in alignment with our true selves and purpose. (To learn how to effectively protect your energy from such conditioning, read my book *Protect Your Light*.)

As a result, our "I," our consciousness and sense of will are to a great degree influenced by other people and systems whose will was either instilled into us, or is stronger than ours. This means that many of the desires we're working on manifesting aren't in alignment with our purpose and highest good; in fact, they're not really *our* desires. They belong to the people and systems we listened to our entire lives.

From this perspective, our sense of self or "me"—our thoughts, emotions, likes and dislikes, hobbies and interests—and the ideas and desires we nurture and strive to manifest aren't really about what *we* want for us, but about what *others* want for us.

Reclaiming Your Authentic Desires

Since our mental masculine energy, our "I" or will, and therefore our desires, are to a great degree guided by our conditioning, an essential pillar of the manifestation process has to do with doing the inner work. We have to do the work of deprogramming our minds from the limiting thoughts, fears, beliefs, and conditioning we've been indoctrinated with, and realigning ourselves with the thoughts, beliefs, and desires that our higher self has for us.

In other words, manifestation isn't just about doing the high-vibe work, but also about having the courage to face your deepest, darkest fears and limiting beliefs. It's about stopping being in denial of your shadow self, and using processes to heal, resolve, and transmute the darkness into light. It's only when we dive deep and strip the layers of our conditioning that we can allow our true desires and purpose to come to the surface.

Unfortunately, the majority of manifestation literature teaches spiritual bypassing. Thus, you've been guided to ignore your fears and limiting beliefs and avoid facing your negative emotions. Instead, you've been asked to *just* "think positive," "raise your vibration," and "fake it till you make it." But how can you think positive when you have deep-seated limiting beliefs around negativity? How can you raise your vibration when you have unresolved traumas that keep you rooted in fear? How can you fake it till you make it when you've been conditioned to see yourself in a limited way?

Ignoring the negative and focusing on the positive may work in the short term, and you may find yourself enjoying some ephemeral manifestation bliss. But eventually, your buried, unhealed fears and limiting beliefs will gain momentum, take over your consciousness, and sabotage the manifestation process.

The law of gender marks the end of Part One of the book. Now that you have a deeper understanding of the seven manifestation laws of the Universe, you're ready to start living them. In the next part, you'll learn how to use these laws in a practical manner to manifest your desires and purpose.

2

LIVING THE LAWS

9

FIVE-STEP MANIFESTATION PROCESS

"The possession of knowledge, unless accompanied by a
manifestation and expression in action, is like the hoarding of
precious metals—a vain and foolish thing. Knowledge, like wealth, is
intended for use. The Law of Use is universal, and he who violates it
suffers by reason of his conflict with natural forces."
—The Kybalion

All seven manifestation laws of the Universe have practical application. Here in Part Two of the book, I've organized their practical component in a five-step process that you can use to manifest your desires and purpose.

Rather than a quick formula for instant manifestation, this five-step process is, instead, a long-term framework for your manifestation journey, that you get to use and improve on throughout your life. Therefore, use the practices in the five-step process consistently, to inspire, reorganize, and optimize your manifestation practice, so that you make conscious manifestation a part of who you are and what you do.

Here are the five steps to the manifestation process:

1. Raise Your Vibration
2. Clarify Your Desires
3. Release Your Limiting Beliefs
4. Nurture the Energy of Your Desires
5. Take Inspired Action

To begin with, you'll start by raising your overall vibrational frequency so that you can be a match to the vibration of the Universe and your inner being. As your vibration rises, you'll be able to receive guidance as to the desires that are aligned to your life purpose, rather than desires drawn from your ego and a state of disconnection from your true self. Simultaneously, your high vibration will bring you into alignment with your desires so you can immediately start the process of manifesting them.

When we start raising our vibration and following our purpose, we trigger fears and limiting beliefs that come up to sabotage the process. At this stage of the manifestation journey, you'll learn how to proactively identify and release the fears and limiting beliefs that keep you stuck.

The fourth step of the process involves nurturing the energy of your desires. You'll learn powerful energetic processes to turn your desires and yourself into powerful vibrational magnets that attract supportive people, spirit guides, and other cooperative components to bring your desires and purpose to life. This process goes beyond raising your overall vibration to raising the vibration of your specific desires too.

The final step of the process has to do with balancing your masculine and feminine energy, so you can receive inspired guidance as to the action steps you need to take to bring your desires to life. You'll learn the importance of becoming a cooperative component in the manifestation process, and joining the Universe in a collaborative effort to manifest your desires.

Meditation Prep Process

Many of the upcoming manifestation practices will take you on deep meditation journeys. Before you engage in these meditations, it's important that you follow the meditation prep process of relaxing, centring, and grounding.

All three steps are of vital importance for both the effectiveness of the processes and your safety when practising these meditations.

Relaxation

The key to a successful meditation lies in achieving complete relaxation of both your mind and body. The guided visualizations you'll practise will take you on inner journeys, enabling you to connect with spiritual energies and engage with the spiritual realm. This necessitates a gentle surrender of your physical presence, allowing your inner essence to assume control, a state facilitated by conscious relaxation.

To begin with, sit or lie down in a comfortable position, close your eyes, and take a deep breath. Continue by relaxing the top of your head, and then gently progress downward, covering every inch of your body. Avoid rushing this process; instead, concentrate on fully relaxing each body part, i.e., your eyes, cheeks, and jaw.

Once you've reached the soles of your feet, take three deep breaths, exhaling as if you're transforming into a limp, wet noodle. I've discovered this visualization to be highly effective in releasing any lingering physical tension, allowing complete surrender.

With your body at ease, turn your attention to calming your mind. It may be challenging to completely empty your mind of thoughts, so provide it with something small to focus on, such as the rhythmic ticking of a clock or the steady beat of your heart. Should random thoughts intrude, acknowledge them briefly and then gently release them. The objective is to minimize mental chatter as much as possible.

Centring

Centring is about ensuring that all your bodies—your physical, mental, emotional, and other subtle bodies—occupy the same space within you. Frequently, our physical body may be physically present, but our mind drifts elsewhere, and our emotions reside in a different place altogether. When we're not centred, our energy field weakens, leaving us susceptible to energetic and spiritual disturbances.

Follow these steps to centre yourself:

1. Find a comfortable seated position and gently close your eyes.

2. Inhale deeply through your nose, allowing the breath to descend into your belly, then exhale completely until your lungs are empty.

3. Check in with your physical body to ensure it's relaxed and not holding on to any tension. If you notice tension, use the wet noodle process taught above to relax your body fully.

4. Once your physical body is fully at ease, turn your mental gaze to your emotional body, the second layer of your aura, which is essentially your emotional core. With each breath, focus on your prevailing emotions, simply acknowledging them and allowing them to be. Acknowledging them is enough to centre your emotional body.

5. Shift your attention to the mental body, the third layer of your aura, and follow the same process. Acknowledge any thoughts that arise in your mind, and then allow them to pass without attachment.

6. Envision the remaining four layers of your aura, the spiritual layers, using your mind's eye. These layers may be a bit more elusive, but all you need to do to centre them is to continue breathing while visualizing them naturally arranging themselves around your physical body.

7. Mindfully recognize all seven layers, or bodies, of your aura. Now, direct your focus to the centre of your heart and visualize your heart chakra acting as a magnetic force, drawing all seven layers toward it. Your heart, as the point of convergence between your physical and spiritual aspects, serves as the anchor for your centred state.

8. Once you sense that you are fully present, centred, and focused, take a few more deep breaths and gently open your eyes.

Grounding

Grounding is the practice of establishing an energetic link with the earth, and it's important for several key reasons:

Firstly, the earth is a powerful energy protector. When you ground yourself, you tap into its stabilizing energy, which grants you greater control over your own energy. Secondly, maintaining this connection during meditation offers a continuous flow of vital life-force energy, which purifies and recalibrates your energy field. Lastly, having an energetic tie to the earth allows excess energy that your body cannot manage to dissipate, preventing overwhelm during meditation journeys and facilitating your ability to comprehend and interpret the insights you receive.

Follow these steps to ground yourself:

1. Find a comfortable seated position and gently close your eyes.
2. After achieving a centred state, shift your focus to your root chakra, located at the base of your spine. You can imagine it as a radiant sphere of ruby-red light. This chakra governs your connection to the physical world and the earth, making it the primary chakra for grounding.
3. Visualize an energetic cord extending from your root chakra, descending deep into the earth beneath you. Envision this cord delving through layers of soil, passing caverns and crystalline mountains, and penetrating the earth's crust, finally reaching the core, resembling a massive red crystal.
4. Allow this cord to naturally wrap itself securely around the earth's core, mirroring the appearance of your own root chakra.
5. With your connection to the earth's core established, visualize all stress, tension, and negativity flowing out of your various bodies through this cord, into the earth. Imagine this energy being absorbed and transformed by the earth. At the same time, envision

healing and grounding energy from the earth ascending through the cord into your physical body, revitalizing and grounding you.

6. Maintain this state for as long as it feels appropriate, and, when you're ready to conclude, take deep breaths as you gradually open your eyes, experiencing a sense of groundedness and vitality.

STEP 1

Raise Your Vibration

10

YOUR DAILY HAPPINESS PRACTICE

As discussed in Chapter 4, the law of vibration or attraction states that to manifest your desires you need to raise your frequency to match the frequency of already having that desire. Additionally, by raising your vibration to match the frequency of the Universe, you automatically become a vibrational match to all of your desires, and let them come into your life effortlessly and at the right time.

There are many processes to quickly raise your vibration, but in this chapter I'll teach you a framework that you can use to optimize your lifestyle so that it fosters a consistently high-vibrational state. Remember, it's your overall vibration that the Universe responds to, rather than your ephemeral, moment-by-moment emotions. Therefore, it's important to reorganize your life so that it supports and amplifies a high-vibrational frequency.

Creating Your Daily Happiness Practice

Happiness isn't something you get, but something you allow and remember. Since you're a physical extension of the Universe, and since the Universe vibrates at the frequency of happiness, then by definition your true essence is also the vibration of happiness. This is something you experienced when you were a baby, but, as you grew up and experienced the complications of life, you eventually forgot.

Your daily happiness practice is a way for you to remember and return to your innate happiness. Essentially, it consists of a group of practices that you commit to doing on a daily basis, for the purpose of consciously nurturing your alignment to the Universe and your true self. Having a daily happiness practice will help polarize you to the vibration of happiness throughout the day, so that you can neutralize the emotional rhythm of the emotional pendulum—the inevitable ups and downs of life.

The happiness practice is usually referred to as the spiritual practice, but I like to call it a happiness practice because spirituality is simply a journey to reconnecting with our true spiritual essence, which is the vibration of happiness.

To craft your happiness practice, all you need to do is pick three activities that help you nurture the vibration of happiness and do them on a daily basis, ideally at the start of your day. Rather than just focusing on traditionally spiritual practices, choose any practices that nurture the emotion of happiness.

Here's a list of practices to inspire you:

▷ Meditate

▷ Write ten things you're grateful for

▷ Play with your pets

▷ Put on loud music and dance

▷ Sing your heart out

▷ Connect with nature

▷ Read a book that inspires you

▷ Watch something motivational

▷ Exercise

▷ Do a mini ritual

▷ Pray

▷ Do positive affirmations in the mirror

▷ Journal about your dreams and desires

As soon as you've picked your three activities, commit to doing them daily and for at least 15 minutes in total. The reason it's important to be consistent with your happiness practice, and spend a good amount of time at it, is that happiness is a muscle that needs to be nurtured; and, nurturing requires momentum. Our lives have become increasingly busy and demanding, and there are so many factors that can get us out of alignment, at any point. A five-minute happiness practice will likely not be enough to polarize you to the vibration of happiness, and you'll likely find yourself being swayed by the first challenge that comes your way.

Conversely, when you commit to spending a sizeable amount of time nurturing the vibration of happiness, you create a strong enough momentum of that vibration to make you emotionally resilient to the various factors that can mess up your vibration throughout the day. As a result, your daily happiness practice polarizes your vibration to the emotion of happiness, so you can effectively neutralize negative states and emotions as they come your way.

That being said, it's also important to allow your happiness practice to shift and change as you do. I first started doing my happiness practice consistently in 2012 and since then it's taken many shapes and forms. At first, and while I was a university student and had more free time in the mornings, it consisted of guided meditations, positive affirmations, journaling, and a mini oracle card reading for some daily inspiration. When I eventually got my first full-time job in London my practice was limited to a 15-minute meditation in the morning, as that was all the available time I had. Eventually, when I quit my full-time job, moved back to Cyprus, and went fully self-employed, I expanded my happiness practice to a three-hour practice that included yoga, meditation, ritual, EFT tapping, and journaling.

As you, your life, and your lifestyle change, your happiness practice should also change to support your new circumstances. If you stubbornly try to maintain the same practice no matter your life changes, it can end up feeling stifling and be counterproductive to helping you nurture a high vibration.

As you change, your likes and interests may change, too. Activities that previously excited you may eventually lose their appeal, and spiritual practices that helped you feel connected to the Universe may no longer do so. Therefore, it's always a good idea to be mindful of how your happiness practice makes you feel on a daily basis and make adjustments as and when needed. As a rule of thumb, I like to review my happiness practice every three to six months, to keep it fresh and uplifting.

PRO TIP

While your happiness practice should be a daily priority, there will come days when for whatever reason you won't be able to complete it. For these occasions, it's a good idea to have an emergency happiness practice. This consists of a stripped-down version of your happiness practice, and is the bare minimum you need to maintain your existing vibrational state. Your emergency practice can be between 5 and 15 minutes and include a single activity that'll give you the most result in the least amount of time. For me, this is a ten-minute mindfulness meditation. What does it for you?

TAKE ACTION

Take out your journal and brainstorm activities you can add to your daily happiness practice. Choose the three most fun ones, and schedule at least 15 minutes to practise them every morning.

Transmuting with Gratitude

Your daily happiness practice will set the tone of your day to a high-vibe one, and you'll likely be able to maintain that for most of the day. However, as your day unfolds you may interact with people and spaces, have experiences and encounter challenges that will inevitably lower your vibration. On such occasions, you'll need to have an action plan for transmuting the negative emotions or experiences and restoring your high vibration.

There are many complex modalities and processes you can use to transmute negative emotions and experiences. Personally, I like to use something quick and simple as I go through my day, and reserve the more intricate practices for when I have the time and space to do the deeper inner work. For this reason, my go-to process for transmuting any situation that lowers my vibration throughout the day is gratitude.

Gratitude is a transmuting emotion. It allows you to alchemize negative states to more positive ones, by shifting your perspective and searching for the silver lining. Whatever it is you may be going through that's messing up your vibration, you can use gratitude in an intentional and creative way to find something that'll make you feel better about it. Instead of pretending that all is well when it really isn't, being grateful allows you to search for a real reason to feel good, which helps alleviate the stress and tension of the situation so you can resolve it faster.

For example, if your car breaks down while driving to work you can be grateful for the extra time you get to spend by yourself, or that you have someone to come and pick you up. If you lose your phone, you can be grateful for the social media break you'll get as a result.

Gratitude Touchstones

The way I use gratitude as a mental transmutation tool is by scheduling gratitude touchstones throughout the day. These are short sessions of gratitude that I practise at different times in my day, and which function as mindful reminders to intentionally transmute any negative situations that may have come up.

Specifically, I have three gratitude touchstones every day: one at the start of the day, one in the middle of the day, and the final one at the end of the day. Each one of them has a different purpose. The first touchstone forms part of my daily happiness practice, and its purpose is twofold. Firstly, it serves as one of my three practices of raising my vibration and setting the tone of my day. Secondly, it serves as a way for me to transmute any negative emotions or situations that may have come up early in the morning, or negative thoughts that have come up in my mind. By tackling them before the day progresses, I prevent them from escalating and lowering my vibration later on in the day.

My second gratitude touchstone, for the middle of my day, serves the purpose of allowing me to be grateful for all the positive things that happened so far in the day, but also to transmute any negative situation or emotion that may have come up. Whether something went wrong at work, or if I had an argument with a friend or encountered a difficult client, I use the second touchstone to find the silver lining of the situation and feel grateful about it.

Finally, I have the last touchstone, at the end of the day. This is an opportunity to express my gratitude for all the great things I've experienced during the day, and to transmute any negative experiences I haven't had the chance to resolve yet. As a result, I end my day at the same high-vibrational state I started it, if not higher, since by that point I've had two additional sessions during which I have intentionally amplified my vibration with gratitude.

Essentially, having three gratitude touchstones throughout your day will help you to either elevate your frequency if things have been running smoothly for you, or maintain your existing frequency by resolving situations that can lower it.

There are many ways to express your gratitude during your touchstones. You may write things down in your journal, speak them out loud to yourself, or just think about them. However, my favourite way of doing so is by sending voice messages to my best friends.

I first started doing this after practising Gala Darling's Magical Morning Practice process from her book *Radical Radiance*, and I've since adjusted it to work for me. When you send your gratitude practice as a voice message to a friend, you get the added benefit of having someone listen, think about, and comment on what you're saying, which amplifies the vibration of your offering. Additionally, if your friend chooses to do the practice with you, listening to their gratitude practice inspires yours, and adds to the things you're grateful for.

TAKE ACTION

Decide on the format of your three gratitude touchstones— writing, speaking them out to yourself, or sending a voice message to a friend—and commit to doing them daily, for as long as it's fun.

11

OPTIMIZE YOUR HIGH-VIBE LIFESTYLE

Your daily happiness practice and gratitude touchstones will help you set and maintain a high vibrational frequency throughout your day—for the most part. To sustain the vibration you nurture in these practices, you need to optimize your lifestyle to support it. For the purpose of raising your vibration, your lifestyle involves primarily your diet, fitness routine, your relationships, and the vibrational state of your house; and these are the areas we'll be focusing on in this chapter.

Often, we place too much emphasis on using energetic and spiritual processes for raising our vibration, and forget that every single choice we make, whether it is "spiritual" or not, affects our vibration. In this chapter, I'll help you assess the vibrational quality of your lifestyle, and provide you with guidelines to optimize it.

High-Vibe Lifestyle Wheel

The high-vibe lifestyle wheel is a visual way to assess the vibrational quality of the different aspects of your lifestyle, so you know where you most need to focus on. The wheel includes the five main lifestyle areas of Food, Fitness, Hobbies & Activities, Relationships, and Home. In each category you'll see a scale of 1–10, signifying the overall vibrational frequency of each life area (1 has the lowest vibration and 10 has the highest vibration).

To assess the vibrational quality of your lifestyle, use your colouring pencils or pens to colour each area up to the number that feels true to you currently. For example, if you do a great job at maintaining high-vibe relationships, then you could colour in the Relationships area up to the number 8 or 9, but if you need more work on decluttering your house then you may give the house section a score of 2 or 3.

Once you've coloured in your wheel, read the guidance provided in the following sections to get ideas on improving each area, and use your journal to brainstorm an action plan.

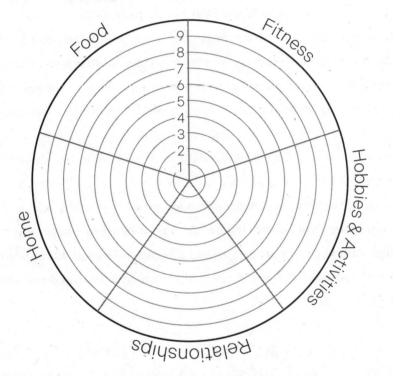

Food and Fitness

Your body is the physical vessel your soul chose to inhabit in this lifetime. It's your soul manifested in physical form so that it can live comfortably within this time–space reality. Therefore, to keep your vibration consistently high you need to go beyond just practising spiritual processes and ensure that your physical body feels high-vibe too.

I'm not a doctor or nutritionist, thus I'm not qualified to give you advice on nutrition, exercise, or physical health. Rather than advise you, I'll instead share the framework I use to make healthy choices for *my* body, so you can do your own research and come up with the best plan for you. The following guidance is meant to inspire your journey and give you general guidelines on what I feel is important to keep your body healthy and its vibration high.

Choose Food that Feeds Your Soul

The number one rule I live by when it comes to keeping the vibration of my body high is that everyone's body is different; therefore, there are no rules that work for everyone. Instead, my guidance has always been to listen to my body's messages and adjust my diet and exercise habits accordingly.

When I was first starting out on my spiritual path, I felt guided to become vegetarian. I'd been an avid meat-eater for years, but after a week-long vegetarian challenge I'd found myself feeling lighter, healthier, and better than I'd ever felt before. So, I decided to become vegetarian (pescatarian, to be accurate) and I'd been so for seven years. As soon as I'd moved back to Cyprus, I could feel my body craving meat again. Rather than judging or resisting this, I once again listened to my body and transitioned to a Mediterranean diet that included a balance of meat, fish, and vegetables.

Each time I listened to my body rather than blindly follow someone else's guidance about what's right or wrong, I was rewarded with better health, a higher vibration, and a boost to my psychic abilities.

TAKE ACTION

What foods raise your vibration? What foods deplete it? Keep a food diary for a week, noting what you eat and when, as well as the way your body feels after each meal. Use this as guidance to make positive changes to your diet.

Work Out to Feel Good

I believe that exercise is essential for keeping our vibration high. From a scientific perspective, when we exercise our body releases chemicals called endorphins, which trigger a positive feeling in the body, thus raising our vibration. Energetically, when your muscles break down after exercise so they can grow back stronger, your body literally calls for life-force energy to facilitate this process, which also raises your vibration.

That being said, since every body is different there's no one exercise that's right for everyone. Over the years, as I've lived in different countries and hung out with different people, I've found myself being influenced by the popular exercise habits in these places. In London, I felt pressure to run in parks even though I hate running. In Spain, everyone was into cycling, which I find boring. In Cyprus, people are obsessed with working out at the gym, looking all buff and having a six-pack. What's the exercise trend where you live? Have you ever felt pressure to follow along, even though you don't particularly enjoy it?

I eventually decided that, instead of following the trends, I'd exercise for the purpose of feeling good and looking good on *my* terms. For me, this has meant trying a variety of workout routines, such as yoga and flexibility training, taking salsa and commercial dance classes, hiking in nature, swimming in the sea, and weightlifting in the gym. As a result, I don't exercise just because I know it's good for my health and vibration; I exercise because I enjoy every moment of it.

TAKE ACTION

What type of exercises do you enjoy doing? What do you not enjoy? Use your journal to brainstorm possible enjoyable exercise routines, and give them a try within the next month. Once you've found what works for you, commit to exercising three to four times a week.

Hobbies and Interests

By definition, your hobbies and interests are activities that interest you and help raise your vibration. More than that, our hobbies and interests, especially the ones we had as children, are directly aligned with our life purpose. The emotion of happiness is aligned with the life purpose, so that, whenever we do something that makes us feel happy, we're simultaneously following our life purpose.

In my experience, we tend to have many and different types of hobbies when we're younger, but, as we grow up and our lives get more complicated, we eventually let most of them go and prioritize other things. When we're children we dream of making our hobbies and interests our careers, but these dreams are quickly smothered by fear-based beliefs and societal indoctrination. As a result, we let our passions go and settle for the safe career choices that we were promised would give us the happiness we wished for.

Later on in life, after we've followed the soul-less career path we were directed towards but haven't found the fulfilment we were promised, we start searching for our happiness where we left it: in our hobbies and interests.

For the most part of my life, I was passionate about performing. I sang, danced, and acted, and dreamed of one day becoming a musical theatre actor. Eventually, when I realized that my passion for spirituality was stronger than my passion for performing, I completely abandoned theatre and focused solely on building my spiritual business.

Eight years later, after publishing my first two books and having built a successful business, I found myself missing something. Although I'd been undertaking all kinds of spiritual processes to keep my vibration high, there was an underlying sadness that I couldn't shake off. When I tuned in, I was surprised to find out that I'd missed performing! Yes, spirituality was my purpose, but so was performing.

After that, I signed up for singing and dancing classes, and at the time of writing this chapter I'm on my second year of drama school! Rekindling my passion for performing filled in the emptiness I'd felt and drastically raised my vibration.

TAKE ACTION

What are your current hobbies and interests? Do you have any, or have you abandoned them at some point in your life? Use your journal to ponder these questions and come up with a list of activities you enjoy doing. Commit to giving at least two of these activities a try, and notice how they affect your vibration.

Relationships

If you want to find out what your dominant vibrational frequency is like, look at the people you surround yourself with. Look at your partner, your friends, family, colleagues, acquaintances, and even the strangers you interact with on a daily basis. The people in our life are always in alignment with our vibrational frequency, otherwise the law of vibration wouldn't have brought them into our lives in the first place.

With this in mind, consider the degree to which the people around you represent the high-vibe life you wish to have. Are the people around you mostly positive, happy, and fulfilled? Or are they leaning towards negativity, sadness, and pessimism? I know this may sound quite harsh but, if the people around you don't embody the high vibration you wish to have, then you should consider whether they still belong in your life. If you're serious about making a high-vibe life your priority, then you need to ensure that you're surrounded by people who support and amplify your vibration, rather than deplete it.

If you've been low-vibe for a long period of time, then you have naturally attracted people on that same vibrational frequency. Now that you're ready to turn over a new leaf and consistently raise your vibration, you'll find that you'll no longer resonate with this old group of people anyway. Ending or transitioning these relationships will set both of you free to find new people who match who you want to be.

The reason we're hesitant about ending relationships is because we don't know how to do so gracefully. You see, we spend so much time learning how to create fulfilling relationships but so little time learning how to end them. I've learned this the hard way. Not knowing how to end relationships gracefully as a teenager and young adult, I simply ghosted the people I wanted to distance myself from, which was disrespectful at best and deeply hurtful at worst.

Gradually, I've learned to end relationships in a graceful and assertive way, that respects both my and their emotions. I've learned to be OK with having difficult conversations, to talk with compassion, and to end relationships while still honouring the time and experiences we have spent together. To learn my practical framework and energetic process of releasing relationships, read my book *Protect Your Light*.

TAKE ACTION

Make a list of the people in your life who lower your vibration, or who you no longer resonate with. Write down a script of the conversation you can have to end or transition these relationships, while respecting both their and your emotions. When the time is right, have these conversations to respectfully end the relationships.

House

I've always been fascinated with the way physical space holds energy. Feng shui, the Chinese modality of harmonizing space, was the first spiritual modality I ever practised, when I was 15. Later on, my university thesis in human geography was all about space and memory, and how our experiences become energetically imprinted on the physical space we live in. Finally, in my training as an Elemental Space Clearing® practitioner with Denise Linn, I learned how to consciously cleanse the energy of spaces and infuse them with new, positive energy.

What my 15-plus-year journey of studying the energy of spaces has taught me is that the physical space we live in unequivocally affects our vibration. Unless cleansed, your house stores different types of negative energy attachments in its ether, which change the vibration of the space, and therefore yours too. Such toxic energy attachments include "predecessor energy" from the house's previous inhabitants, your own residual energy you've released while living there, energy from charged objects you've bought, been gifted or inherited, low-level spirits, and more.

Additionally, items you haven't used for a while, that you no longer love, or which no longer represent who you've become, hold stagnant energy that lower the vibration of the space they're in. This is why decluttering is such a popular and powerful practice. If you've ever watched one of the many decluttering TV shows, you'll notice that people end up decluttering not just their house, but instead having a whole-life transformation. This is because by decluttering they, literally, let go of energies and past identities that held them back, and then they're free to make positive changes in their lives.

As a result, to support your journey of living a high-vibe life it's important to regularly declutter and cleanse the energy of your house. When you do so effectively, you not only create a space that helps you maintain your high vibration, but you also let your space support you in raising your vibration further.

To learn an easy process for decluttering your house read my book *Be The Guru*, and to learn how to cleanse the energy of your space read my book *Protect Your Light*.

TAKE ACTION

Make a list of all the rooms in your house. Rate their vibration on a scale of 1 to 10, with 10 being the highest vibration. Brainstorm ways to regularly declutter and cleanse them, to raise their vibration.

12

TRANSMUTE NEGATIVE EMOTIONS

In Chapter 4 I introduced the emotional guidance scale, as taught by Abraham-Hicks. This scale shares the 22 main emotions we experience as humans based on their vibrational frequency. Although there are many more emotions that we may experience, this scale provides a basic framework that can help us identify where we are at, and where we can go to. At the lowest vibrational frequency, we have fear, grief, desperation, despair, and powerlessness, and at the highest vibrational frequency we find joy, appreciation, empowerment, freedom, and love.

As you go through life, you'll find yourself at different points on this scale. Even though if you follow the guidance in the previous few chapters you'll be able to consistently nurture the emotions at the top of the scale, you're only human. There will come moments when something happens that throws you off your game, that not even your gratitude touchstones can help you break through. This is where the following process comes into play, to help you resolve persistent negative emotions and transmute them to more positive ones.

Understanding Negative Emotions

All negative emotions want is to be heard and acknowledged, and as soon as they've done so they lose their power and we're able to feel more positive emotions. This is why expressing our emotions by venting, journaling, or crying works so well in releasing them. Don't you always feel better after you've expressed your negative emotion in one or more of these ways?

There are many processes you can use to release and transmute negative emotions; some of them are guided practices and modalities such as

Emotional Freedom Technique (EFT), and others are simpler processes such as having a cathartic cry. Having tried many practices and modalities over the years, I've come to understand that to truly transmute negative emotional states we need to go beyond just expressing them, to identifying and desensitizing their root cause.

Think of a negative emotion as a bucket that includes various life experiences and memories during which you'd previously felt that emotion, including the specific experience during which you *first* felt that emotion. These experiences can be thought of as emotional imprints, as they represent the times in your life during which you were imprinted with a specific negative emotion. From this perspective, to fully transmute a present negative emotion, you need to identify and transmute the memory or memories during which you first experienced that emotion.

For example, let's say you have an argument with a colleague at work. In that argument, you've felt that your colleague disrespected you, and you've used the emotional guidance scale to find out that your dominant emotion as a result of this experience was the emotion of anger. You can try to resolve this emotion by venting to a friend, journaling about it, or using EFT, but, although you'll feel better afterwards, you likely won't resolve the root cause of that emotion. As a result, next time you get into an argument and feel disrespected, the anger will resurface.

Conversely, by identifying the first significant experience, or number of experiences, during which you were imprinted with the emotion of anger, you're given the opportunity to release the basis for feeling angry each time you're disrespected.

Integral Eye Movement Therapy

Integral Eye Movement Therapy (IEMT) is a revolutionary psychotherapy model developed by British neuroscientist Andrew Austin, which aims to release negative emotions by identifying and desensitizing the upsetting memories that created them. Based on the NLP eye-accessing cues and drawing from the Eye Movement Desensitization and Reprocessing (EMDR) modality used successfully in trauma therapy, IEMT is a powerful technique for fully transmuting negative emotions and raising your vibration.

I discovered IEMT in the summer of 2020 after going through an emotional breakdown. Having tried all my usual practices and modalities to no avail, I worked with an IEMT practitioner and in just four sessions I'd healed deep-seated emotions, traumas, and limiting beliefs I'd been working on releasing for years. I was so impressed by the processes that I went ahead and trained in the modality myself. Today, I use IEMT in most of my sessions with clients, as it's by far the most effective method I've discovered for releasing negative emotions.

Inspired by my IEMT training and a desire to delve deeper into the realms of healing trauma and limiting beliefs, I proceeded to train as a clinical trauma specialist and subsequently earned a master's degree in psychology.

In the following exercise, I'll guide you to use IEMT to transmute negative emotions to positive ones. The guidance I provide won't qualify or certify you to practise or teach IEMT, but rather empower you with a new tool you can use to support your manifestation journey. You can read more about learning and training in IEMT at **www.integraleyemovementtherapy.com**.

Transmute Negative Emotions with IEMT

When you identify a strong negative emotion, take some time privately and rate the strength of that emotion on a scale of 1 to 10, with 1 being the weakest and 10 being the strongest expression. It is important to do this right at the beginning, so you can assess the effectiveness of the process later on.

Once you have your score, ask yourself the following question: *When was the first time I remember feeling this way?*

Rather than picking a general time in your life, allow your mind to go back to the first specific memory that comes up. This doesn't need to be the first time you had that emotion, but rather the first time that comes up for you currently.

If no specific memory comes up, you can ask yourself the following:

When was the first time I remember someone else feeling this way?

As soon as you have the specific memory in mind, think about the memory over and over again while moving your eyes for about 30 seconds in the way demonstrated below.

Eye Movement Pattern

With your head aligned straight ahead and your eyes open or closed, start by moving your eyes side to side, all the way to the edges so that you feel a gentle pull of your eye muscles. Make sure that you only move your eyes and not your head.

Then, proceed by moving your eyes diagonally from the top right to the bottom left corner, followed by the other diagonal from the top left to the bottom right corner.

Once you've moved your eyes for about 30 seconds in total while thinking about the specific memory, close your eyes and take two long deep breaths in. When you open your eyes, ask yourself:

How does that memory make me feel now?

Score the emotion from a scale of 1 to 10. You'll likely notice that the intensity of the emotion has decreased significantly.

Additionally, the memory you had may have faded from your mind or seem further away, or you may now have an enlightening understanding of it.

If the emotional score is higher than 3 out of 10, repeat the process once more until it falls to a 3 or below. If the emotional intensity persists to a score of 4 or above, there is likely a stronger memory that you need to work on. If this memory hasn't already naturally come up while you were moving your eyes, go back to the initial questions and dig a little deeper until you've found it.

When you're done with the process, go back to the emotional guidance scale on page 35 and find the new emotion you're at. You'll likely be at a much high-vibrational emotional state, one that you can easily amplify with gratitude and your daily happiness practice.

IEMT Contraindications

IEMT is a safe process to use for most people, but as with all processes there are contraindications to be aware of. Specifically, it's not recommended to use IEMT if any of the following are true:

▷ You are currently suffering from or have a history of psychotic illness.

▷ You have any active or current ocular disease, including conjunctivitis, glaucoma, history of detached retina, or recent trauma such as "a black eye.

▷ You're a victim of or witness to a crime and are likely to be giving evidence in any legal process. IEMT is a method that influences the way memories are recalled and encoded. As a result, the credibility of a testimony from someone who has undergone IEMT treatment might be scrutinized.

Rediscovering the Song in His Heart

When Andreas first sought my help, he was carrying a persistent sadness that had troubled him for years, despite his best efforts in therapy and personal development. He was doing work he loved, was happily married to Jane, and had a loving family. On the surface, everything seemed harmonious, yet beneath it all lay an inexplicable melancholy that he could not understand.

Our sessions began with an attempt to pinpoint the source of his sadness. Using IEMT, we delved into his past and discovered a childhood incident that had left a lasting scar.

As a kid, Andreas had a deep passion for singing. He was actively involved in his school's choir and took part in musicals. However, one day his music teacher publicly humiliated him for forgetting the lyrics during a school performance. This incident filled him with shame and led him to give up singing.

Over the years, Andreas pursued a career in fine art, which, while enjoyable, wasn't his true passion. Little did he know his underlying sadness stemmed from denying his love for singing and veering off his true path.

Throughout our sessions, Andreas gradually started to release the sadness and shame he had carried for years. He decided to face his fear and signed up for singing classes. With each note he sang, he regained a piece of himself that had been dormant for too long. Joining a band and performing regularly at a local bar helped him rekindle his passion.

His journey took another positive turn when he began performing at weddings, sharing in others' happiness while celebrating his own newfound joy.

13

NEUTRALIZE NEGATIVE EMOTIONS

A nother way of transmuting negative emotions is to utilize the laws of polarity and neutralization, and polarize yourself to the positive emotional counterpart of the negative emotion you feel. The law of polarity states that all manifestations, including emotional states, are on a vibrational scale. Therefore, wherever you are on that scale you have access to both its higher and lower vibrational frequencies. You can use the law of neutralization to polarize to a better-feeling emotion when you're feeling low, or elevate your existing, positive emotion when you're feeling great.

Polarizing to a positive emotion when you're feeling a negative emotion is a quick and effective way of raising your vibration. However, if you depend solely on this method for dealing with negative emotions you run the risk of denying or avoiding the root cause of your negative emotional state. The spiritual literature is full of quick fixes for raising our vibration, which, although they work in the short term, don't help us tackle the deep-seated fears and limiting beliefs that are at the core of our low vibration. As a result, they lead to spiritual bypassing, a term coined in the 1980s by John Welwood , defined as the "tendency to use spiritual ideas and practices to sidestep or avoid facing unresolved emotional issues, psychological wounds, and unfinished developmental tasks."

For this reason, it's important that you use this practice, and any other practice for raising your vibration, in combination with the IEMT process in the previous chapter or another process that helps you resolve the underlying issues of your negative emotions. As a rule of thumb, if a negative emotion is both strong and shows up consistently it is likely that there's a deeper issue at play and you need to do some more digging. If a negative emotion feels weaker and only shows up occasionally, then it's likely that there isn't anything serious underlying it, and you can use the following method to neutralize it.

How to Neutralize Negative Emotions

Follow these steps to neutralize any negative emotions you carry:

Step 1—Identify the Negative Emotion

Use the emotional guidance scale from Chapter 4 to pinpoint exactly what emotion it is you're feeling. If it's a long-standing emotional state that requires deeper work, go back to the previous chapter and resolve it using IEMT. If it feels like a weaker and occasional emotion, proceed with the next step.

Step 2—Choose a Higher-Vibrational Emotion

After identifying your negative emotion, search now for a contrasting, higher-vibrational emotion on the scale. It's important to note that the degree to which an emotion is positive or negative is relative. In other words, if you're feeling the emotion of fear then anger is a positive emotion for you. On the other hand, if you're feeling joy then anger would be a negative emotion.

When choosing a contrasting positive emotion, choose one that feels both positive and believable from your current emotional standpoint. To be positive, it has to be at least one step up on the emotional guidance scale from where you are (don't go more than five steps upwards), and to be believable you need to feel that it's possible for you to make that emotional jump given where you are currently.

For example, if you've just lost your job and feel the emotion of unworthiness, you wouldn't want to choose the emotion of joy. Although it's a positive one, you'll likely won't be able to make the emotional jump before passing through a few other emotional states first. Conversely, a positive and believable emotion to choose from the emotion of unworthiness would be anger or disappointment. They're higher-vibrational emotions from your current emotional state, but also believable jumps to make given the context of your experience.

Step 3—Energetic Polarization

Once you've chosen the emotion you want to polarize to, it's important to connect to it energetically first. Every emotion has a specific frequency that you can connect to, so you can access it more easily and effectively. I like to visualize each emotion's frequency as a vibrational cloud that hovers around the Earth's atmosphere and which I can connect to, or disconnect from, using energetic cords of attachment.

To connect to the energetic frequency of your chosen emotion, come into a meditative state by closing your eyes and taking deep breaths. Once you've relaxed your body and centred your energy, visualize an energetic cord extending from your body (you can let the cord choose what part of your body it wants to extend from; it will usually be one of your chakras) and reach out into the Universe, searching for the collective vibrational frequency of your chosen emotion.

Once you've found that frequency, let the energetic cord connect with and hook into it. As soon as you've done so, you'll feel energy flow through from the collective frequency of the emotion, through the energetic cord, to you. You may receive this energy in the form of thoughts, emotions, or simply vibration. Don't second-guess it; trust that the process is taking place.

Stay in this state and receive the transmission of energy for a few minutes. When it feels complete, you can open your eyes and come out of the meditation. Don't cut the cord just yet, as you'll need to be connected to it for the next step of the process.

Step 4—Cognitive Polarization

Now that you've energetically connected with the frequency of your chosen emotion, you can proceed with cognitively polarizing yourself to it. Cognitive polarization has to do with consciously thinking yourself into feeling a specific emotion. You essentially conjure up that emotion by offering specific thoughts that will help you feel it.

With your chosen emotion in mind, ask yourself, "What does this emotion feel like?" over and over again. You can either use your journal to write down what comes to mind, or simply think or speak your thoughts out loud. The aim is to come up with similar-feeling thoughts and emotions that help you both understand and embody the emotion.

Within a few minutes of asking this question, you'll find yourself getting increasingly specific with the thoughts and emotions that come up. As you gain emotional momentum, you'll also find yourself feeling that emotion in relation to what created your original, low-vibrational emotion. This means that you're effectively transmuting the previous emotion and polarizing yourself into the new one. Keep at this process for as long as it takes for you to fully feel and embody your chosen emotion.

Step 5—Cut the Cord and Polarize Upwards

After you've effectively polarized to your chosen emotion, it's time to cut the energetic cord you have to it and start the process again by choosing an even better-feeling emotion. The aim is to polarize higher and higher up the scale until you reach the emotion of joy, right at the top of the scale.

To cut the cord to the existing emotion, simply visualize where this cord extends from on your body, and use your hand as a knife or scissors to cut the cord.

PRO TIP

Once you've neutralized the negative emotion you were feeling and reached the higher-vibrational emotions on the emotional scale, you can add Step 4 of this process to your daily happiness practice. For example, if you've raised your vibration to the emotion of joy then you can consciously nurture that emotion daily by pondering or journaling the question, "What does this emotion feel like?"

Personally, I have a whiteboard in my office that I use to do this practice. I usually write my chosen positive emotion in the centre, focus on the question, and create a tree diagram around it with all the similar-feeling emotions, thoughts, and activities, that come to mind. In no more than 10 minutes I fill up the entire board and fully embody my chosen emotion!

At a point in my life (and when I had more time to spare!), I'd spend hours practising this exercise and reaching higher and higher vibrational states. Nowadays, I have this process in my spiritual toolkit and use it as and when needed.

I call this exercise Focused Magnet of Attraction, and you can read more about it in my book *Be The Guru*.

Montse's Journey from Self-Sabotage to Positivity

When Montse booked a session with me she'd reached breaking point with her own self-sabotaging behaviour, a pattern that had plagued her for as long as she could remember. Her upbringing in a toxic household had left a deep impact on her; she was surrounded by constant complaints from her parents.

Her mother lamented their financial struggles, her exhaustion, and lack of support, while her father grumbled about his job, their cramped living space, and the state of their neighbour. Montse had unwittingly absorbed this negativity and turned it into a habit of her own—she complained about almost everything. It had become so deeply ingrained in her subconscious that she felt powerless to break free from it.

The consequences of her chronic complaining were evident. She constantly felt down and, even when positive events occurred in her life, she had an uncanny ability to find the dark cloud in every silver lining. It was as if she were sabotaging her own happiness, and she desperately wanted to put an end to this self-destructive behaviour but didn't know where to start.

In one of our sessions I recognized that, given her pragmatic nature, Montse needed a gradual approach to address her conditioned negativity. I guided her through a meditation aimed at neutralizing her negative emotions and incrementally elevating her vibrational frequency. The key was to help her shift from lower emotional states to increasingly positive ones, aligning herself with their energy and consciously talking herself into them.

What surprised me most was how effective this process was for Montse. Initially, I had my doubts about whether her deep-rooted negativity would overpower her attempts at raising her emotional state. However, the task of actively talking herself into better-feeling emotions served as a buffer against her ego's resistance and its inclination to sabotage her efforts.

Montse diligently practised this process until she was finally able to shed her habit of complaining. The transformation was remarkable. No longer did she stand in the way of her own happiness. She began to fully embrace and relish the positive experiences that came her way; and, perhaps most importantly, she started to attract even more positivity into her life.

———————⚖———————

14

AMPLIFY POSITIVE EMOTIONS

The law of polarity states that there is no limit to the poles of each manifestation. Therefore, there's no limit to how high or low your vibration can be. In other words, there's no limit to how happy you can be. As you keep on with your daily happiness practice and transmute negative emotions that come up, you'll find your overall vibrational frequency rises higher and higher. You'll eventually reach a state where your life feels high-vibe and you are content most of the time, and as a result your desires will manifest more easily.

It's easy to accept this as it is and settle for a contented life, but why not keep pushing the envelope of your happiness? Why settle for contentment when you can experience ecstasy? Since there's no limit to how high you can raise your vibration, there's also no limit to how much faster or more easily you can manifest something. The process I'll share with you in this chapter will allow you to not just ride, but amplify the upward swing of your high vibration, so you can constantly feel happier and happier.

Polarize Yourself to the Universe

Once you've reached one of the top emotions on the emotional guidance scale—joy, appreciation, empowerment, freedom, or love—you can amplify them by connecting to the frequency of the Universe, which has the highest, and a constantly increasing, vibrational frequency.

When you polarize to the vibration of the Universe, you raise your consciousness to rise above the emotional limits of your ego, and give yourself permission to merge with the frequency of your inner being and Source. This has the added benefit of giving you a broader perspective on your life experience, so that you can more easily neutralize the backward swing of your emotional rhythm and maintain a high vibration, without being negatively affected by life's circumstances.

How to Amplify and Ground Your Positive Emotions

Follow these steps to polarize yourself to the frequency of the Universe:

Step 1—Identify Your Emotional State

The first step of the process is to become aware of your current emotional frequency. This will give you an idea of where you are vibrationally, so you can gauge how much your vibration has increased at the end of the process. To do this, close your eyes and come into a meditative state by relaxing your body and breathing deeply. While you do so, start becoming mindful of how you feel, by paying attention to your body's sensations, thoughts, and feelings. You may use the emotional guidance scale to figure out exactly the emotion you're feeling.

Step 2—Rise through Your Crown Chakra

After you get a sense of your current emotional state, the next step is to raise your consciousness to the frequency of the Universe. To do this you'll work with your crown chakra, which is the energetic portal that facilitates your connection to Source. Your crown chakra is an energy centre found at the top of your head and its colour is pure white or violet.

Focusing your attention on your crown chakra, visualize an energetic channel of white light extending from it and reaching upwards towards the sky, to connect with the frequency of the Universe. Imagine the Universe as a glorious crystalline palace high up in the sky, emanating an ethereal golden light. This crystalline palace doesn't exist in this three-dimensional time–space reality, but is rather a symbolic, vibrational representation of the Universe's frequency so you can more easily connect with it.

Bringing your attention back to your body, visualize your spirit coming out of your physical body and rising up from the crown chakra, through the white channel of light, until it reaches the crystalline palace. While you're rising, you'll feel your vibration rise, too, as you'll be breaking free from the vibrational constraints of your physical body and personality.

Step 3—Bask in the Crystalline Palace

As you enter the crystalline palace, you'll find a beautifully decorated room surrounded by high-vibrational etheric crystals emanating sparkling diamond light. At the centre of this room, you'll see a comfortable armchair made just for you, so that you can sit and soak in the glorious energy.

While on the chair, close your eyes, breathe deeply, and empty your mind. Because you're already at a high-vibrational state of consciousness, you'll find that it's easier to meditate there than it is from within your physical body. Stay there meditating for a while, and let your consciousness be immersed in, and nurtured by, the frequency of the Universe.

Step 4—Ground the New Energy

After a while, and once you feel that your vibration has risen significantly, get out of your meditative state, step out of the crystalline castle, and let your body gradually fall back down into your physical body. As soon as you're back into your body, start bringing some movement into your fingers, wrists, shoulders, and head, and when you're ready open your eyes.

Before you get on with the rest of your day, it's important to ground yourself so that your body assimilates this new vibrational state. To do this, drink some water, touch something physical around you, and do your best to get some physical activity such as walking, running, or another type of exercise.

Ideally, do this exercise for at least 21 days so it can gather momentum and polarize you to a new, high vibrational state. The longer you do it for, the stronger will be your connection to the Universe's frequency and the easier it'll be for you to maintain it and attract experiences that align with it.

As you cross the threshold from one dominant vibrational frequency to the next, your entire life will shift to mirror your inner state. Looking back on my life, I can identify clear vibrational eras that came with their own set of lifestyle, activities, and relationships. Depending on my dominant vibrational frequency at each era, I'd attract people, circumstances, and opportunities that reflected it.

Most importantly, my capacity to withstand life's challenges also depended on my dominant frequency. Year after year, and as I consciously practised this and other practices in the book, I've polarized my vibration so much to the high-vibrational end of the spectrum that I've become incredibly resilient to challenging events and negative emotions. I haven't completely eliminated them from my life—that's not desired or possible —but my connection to the Universal frequency is so strong that I can bounce back quickly.

Grace's Journey from Contentment to Transformation

Working with fellow healers always adds an extra layer of depth to my sessions. They understand energy and how to tap into it, which makes it easier to collaborate in creating profound change. Grace, a talented psychic healer herself, was no exception.

Grace reached out to me not because she was dissatisfied with her life or work; in fact, she was quite content with her current situation and the path she was on. However, she found herself at a point where contentment had plateaued into stagnation. Life felt stable but unexciting. She was ready to ascend to a new level, but she couldn't find the way forward.

While connecting with her energy, it became evident that Grace didn't require a typical psychic clearing session. Her energy field was crystal clear; it merely needed activation. To propel her beyond the emotional and energetic stagnation, she needed an energetic attunement.

I guided Grace through a process of tapping into the boundless energy of the Universe by connecting to the crystalline palace. She was already familiar with this frequency, often utilizing it during her own healing sessions. However, she had yet to incorporate it into her daily spiritual practice. This simple shift became a game-changer for her.

The results were nothing short of remarkable. After our last session, Grace embarked on a transformative journey. She authored not one but two books, launched a successful online course, and ventured on a global journey, travelling and sharing her work with people worldwide.

STEP 2

Clarify Your Desires

15

FIND YOUR PURPOSE AND CHOOSE
ALIGNED DESIRES

After raising your dominant vibrational frequency for some time, you'll be more equipped to receive the desires that are aligned to your purpose, soul contracts, and collective manifestation. Your high vibrational frequency will have aligned you to your inner being and Universal wisdom, both of which are already aware of the aforementioned factors and know the perfect path for you to follow and fulfil your purpose. Simultaneously, by the law of correspondence your high vibration gives you access to the mental and spiritual planes of existence, so you can receive further guidance on clarifying and manifesting your desires.

Although at this point, you're still being held back, to some degree, by fears and limiting beliefs related to your conditioning, your consistently high vibration is sufficient to help you receive the right set of desires for you at this point on your path. As soon as you've clarified these desires, in subsequent chapters we'll work on releasing the specific fears and limiting beliefs related to them.

How to Receive Your Desires

In my book *Lightworkers Gotta Work*, I share a step-by-step, cognitive focused process for finding and defining your life purpose. In this chapter, I'll introduce an energetic approach to doing so, as well as the specific desires aligned to it.

Continue with the following six steps, from creating a cord to the crystalline palace, through to identifying the desires aligned with your soul purpose, to receive your desires.

Step 1—Create a Cord to the Crystalline Palace

After getting centred and grounded, visualize an energetic cord extending from your crown chakra at the top of your head and reaching up to the sky to connect with the frequency of the Universe, which you can imagine as the crystalline palace you connected with in the previous chapter. The aim here is to raise your vibration and anchor to the frequency of Source, so that you can easily download your purpose and desires.

As soon as you make the connection, you'll have direct access to the spiritual beings and your own spirit guides on the spiritual plane of existence. Mentally, call upon your spirit team to come in and facilitate the energetic transmission of your purpose and desires though your established energetic cord. You'll then feel energy flow from the crystalline palace through this cord and into your crown chakra and whole being. Spend a few minutes allowing this transmission to happen naturally.

Step 2—Direct the Energy through Your Chakras

When we receive guidance, ideas, or inspiration from the Universe, there's an energetic pathway this guidance follows through our body, so that it manifests in our lives. Firstly, an idea enters our energy field through our crown chakra. As it moves down to our third-eye chakra, we receive intuitive messages that help us develop and expand that idea mentally. From then, the energy moves down to our throat chakra, which helps us express it to ourselves and others.

Subsequently it moves down to our heart chakra, where it gets infused with our love and passion for it, before it enters the solar plexus chakra, which gives us the confidence and motivation to start working towards it. The idea then makes its way down to the sacral chakra, where it becomes embodied and gets ready to be birthed into the world. Finally, it grounds itself in our root chakra and the earth, after which it finally manifests into our life and the world.

In the second step of this process, you consciously guide the energetic transmission of your purpose and desires through this energetic pathway, so that you can more easily become aware of them, and also to speed up their manifestation.

After taking some time to bask in the energy of your purpose and desires that you've received from the crystalline palace, now consciously direct this energy through your seven chakras. Starting at the crown chakra and moving downwards, let the energy stay in each chakra for at least 30 seconds, so that it's fully metabolized. As the energy moves through your chakras you may feel different sensations within your body. This is normal; it's your body's way of processing the energy and adjusting to these vibrational shifts.

Step 3—Ground the Energy to the Earth

After the energy has been metabolized in your root chakra, the next step is to extend an energetic cord from your root chakra and into the earth. You should already have an energetic cord grounding you to the earth's core from the grounding process you learned in Chapter 9, so let this energy flow through your earth cord until it reaches the centre of the earth. Stay in this state for at least 30 more seconds to allow the energy to be fully grounded.

The reason you ground the energy to the earth is so that you can allow this abstract energy and ideas flowing in from the Universe to easily translate into specific thoughts, words, goals, and action steps. Often, we're good at receiving guidance from Source as energy, but we have a hard time understanding it and explaining it to ourselves and others. This is because we haven't allowed the energy to be metabolized by all our chakras and to ground into the earth.

Finally, call upon the spiritual beings of the mineral and elemental planes of existence to step in and support you. As mentioned previously, the elementals are master manifestors and experts in turning thought into matter. Ask them to support you in manifesting your desires and purpose, and even infuse your earth cord with their energetic qualities, to speed up the manifestation process.

Step 4—Integrate the Energy

By this point, you've established a one-way energetic transmission of your purpose and desires from the Universe, through your chakra system, and to the centre of the earth. Through each step of the process, the energy has developed and matured. It's now ready to return from the earth and into your body, so you can translate it into knowledge.

With intention, visualize the energy of your desires and purpose at the core of the earth start making its way up, to infuse your body and aura. As soon as you do this, you'll have created a cyclical flow of energy, from the Universe to the earth, and from the earth to your body. As this balanced energy integrates within your body and being, it'll inform every piece of consciousness within you of your purpose and desires, so that you can receive them clearly.

Step 5—Define Your Life Purpose

As soon as you've integrated the energy, gently come out of the meditation. You're ready to define your life purpose. Start by getting your journal out or opening a document on your computer, and free-write your answers to the following questions. It's important that you don't think too hard when answering these, and just write whatever comes to mind, even if it doesn't make sense in the beginning. Your ego will want to come in and sabotage what comes through, and by writing freely you'll prevent it from doing so.

Spend at least 15 minutes answering these questions, and do so with as much specificity as possible.

What am I here to do?

Most lightworkers answer this question vaguely, by sharing that they're here to "help people heal" or "make a positive change in the world." While both of these statements are correct, they're part of our collective purpose as lightworkers rather than our specific life purpose. When answering this question, focus on the specific problems you can help resolve or desires you can help fulfil.

Why am I here to do that?

"What's your why?" must be the most clichéd life-coaching question, but there's a reason it's so overly used. Unless you have a strong enough reason to support your life purpose, you'll quickly lose motivation and momentum, and quit. Tune in to your soul and figure out the core drive or motivation behind what you're here to do. What change will your purpose create in the world? What's at stake if you don't follow your purpose?

Who am I here to help?

If you try to help everyone, you'll end up helping no one. This is a business foundation that also applies to life and your purpose. Although your purpose may serve a wide variety of people, you need to identify the specific niche in which you're most passionate about helping. Go beyond generic answers here and figure out the social, psychological, and cultural characteristics of the people who will most benefit from your purpose.

How will I do so?

The how depends on your current and potential expertise. If you're a psychic healer like me, the how may involve writing books, private intuitive readings, healing journeys, and online workshops. What are your specific skills, talents, and knowledge that you can use to support your clients? If you don't have them yet, make a list so you can start learning them.

Where **will I do so?**

Where do you see yourself living your purpose? Is it online or offline? If it's offline, what country, state, or city, do you see yourself in? Or do you see yourself being a nomad and teaching all around the world? If you want to follow your purpose both online and offline, I suggest that you pick the one that feels most exciting to start with; eventually you can expand.

When you're done with the writing, read through your answers and identify the main themes and topics that came up. Spend some more time after that and use your logical mind to flesh out the details, crafting your life purpose declaration in the following format:

I am here to help [who], overcome [what], through [how], in [where], for the purpose of [why].

For example, here's the current definition of my life purpose based on this formula:

"I am here to help lightworkers overcome the fears and limiting beliefs that block them from following their purpose, through spiritual practices, healing journeys, and intuitive guidance, online, for the purpose of creating a ripple effect that creates massive, positive change in the world."

Before you finalize your declaration, check in with your body and intuition to ensure that what you've written feels good to you. Your emotional guidance system is the best judge for this, as your purpose should always inspire the feelings of joy and excitement.

Once you have your life purpose declaration, print or write it on a piece of paper and stick it somewhere where you can read it daily, to keep you aligned and connected with it.

Whether what you've come up with is quite vague or super-specific, it's what you're ready to know about your purpose at this stage of your journey. As you engage with your purpose by taking action towards it, your declaration will also change and become increasingly specific. Thus, it's a good idea to revisit this process every six months to a year.

Step 6—Identify Desires Aligned with Your Life Purpose

Now that you've defined your purpose, you're ready to receive specific desires that are aligned with it. Once you identify these desires, you'll work on manifesting them using the practices in the following chapters. With your life purpose declaration in mind, take out your journal and do a brain dump of all the steps you need to take to follow and fulfil your life purpose. Don't hold back at this stage of the process, but instead let yourself write down all the desires that come to mind.

Once you have your exhaustive list of desires, go through them and choose the ones that feel most exciting and are the easiest ones to manifest first. When choosing desires to manifest, always opt for the ones that not only feel good but from which you can get results fast. Often, choosing bigger desires from the start is a procrastination and self-sabotaging tactic, and can result in giving up and disappointment.

Finally, go through your updated list of desires and choose between three and five desires to focus on while reading this book. Write down your final desires in your journal or on a piece of paper and read them daily so you can maintain your alignment with them. Keep your previous lists to hand so you can revisit them and choose new desires in the future.

Julie's Triumph over Trauma

When I asked Julie about her life's purpose, she initially gave me a response I've heard countless times from those I work with: "I want to help people heal." While this aspiration is noble and shared by many on a spiritual journey, it merely scratches the surface. Defining one's life purpose goes beyond this generic statement; it involves pinpointing the specific demographic one wishes to help and identifying the particular issues or obstacles you can assist them to heal or overcome in this life.

In our session, I explained this concept to Julie and led her through the energetic and cognitive process I share in this chapter, aimed at discovering her specific purpose and aligning it with her desires. By the end of the session, Julie had crafted her life purpose declaration, down to the minutest of details. What she unearthed was a unique talent for helping women to access and heal from past sexual traumas, a path she felt a deep connection and commitment to as a survivor of such trauma herself.

Julie had always been an avid reader of self-help and psychology books on these subjects, but it had never occurred to her that her own past challenges could actually serve as a pathway to helping others heal. In our session, Julie was able to download a series of goals and desires directly aligned with her newfound purpose. Foremost among them was the decision to return to school and pursue a degree in psychotherapy.

I checked in with Julie recently to see how she's been progressing with her goals. Having successfully completed her degree, she then underwent specialized training in trauma therapy. Today she works at a local community centre, where she dedicates her time to guiding women on their journeys toward processing and healing from sexual trauma.

In addition to her hands-on work, Julie is in the process of writing a book, through which she intends to share her personal story and the tools that empowered her own healing journey.

STEP 3

Release Your Limiting Beliefs

16

IDENTIFY YOUR LIMITING BELIEFS

Having raised your overall vibrational frequency and clarified your purpose and desires, the third step to the manifestation process is to identify and release the fears and limiting beliefs that may hinder the manifestation process; what *The Kybalion* refers to as mental transmutation. To understand how fears and limiting beliefs interfere with the manifestation process, you first need to explore where they came from and what their purpose is.

As you come forth into this incarnation you're wholly connected to Source; therefore, you're largely free from fears and limiting beliefs. You're aware of your life purpose and know you can create anything you want. As you grow up and get indoctrinated by your family, the school system, and society, you gradually disconnect from your connection to Source and instead take on fears and beliefs that aren't in alignment with your true nature and purpose.[6]

The people you meet and the experiences you have, shape and strengthen your fears and limiting beliefs, until they gain so much momentum that they take over your reality. As a result of you believing them, you attract people, circumstances, and experiences that back them up, which makes them feel

---

[6] There are also fears and limiting beliefs you inherited from your past lives, but past-life healing goes beyond the scope of this book. That being said, many of the fears and limiting beliefs that come up during this exercise will inevitably be related to your past lives. Working through them using the practices that follow will help you release them to a great degree. To specifically release past-life traumas, fears, and limiting beliefs, check out my online workshops and private sessions at **www.georgelizos.com**.

truer. When you desire something that's not in agreement with your limiting beliefs, your ego—the part of you that's disconnected from Source and has bought into these limiting beliefs—panics and sabotages your desires through resistance, blocking their manifestation.

Here are a few of the most common fears and limiting beliefs that come up when you're ready to start manifesting your desires and purpose:

I'm not good enough.

I need more training.

I don't have time/money to do it.

I'm afraid people will judge me.

If I change too much my friends and family will leave me.

It's been done before.

I could go on. The list of limiting beliefs I hear from people on a daily basis is, truly, endless. When we're confronted with the opportunity to create positive change, our ego pulls out every single trick it has to sabotage the process and keep us stuck in fear and mediocrity. As you do the work of identifying your fears and limiting beliefs in this and subsequent chapters, be aware of this sabotaging tendency and don't let it get in the way of your growth. Instead, use the practices I introduce to tackle these sabotaging beliefs head on.

The Five Whys

The easiest way to identify the fears and limiting beliefs blocking the manifestation of your desires is to ask questions about them and be aware of what comes up, mentally, emotionally, and physically. When we consider a desire that contrasts our current belief system, our mind and body will have a reaction to it. Usually we feel tension in our gut, our heart beats faster, and our mouth dries up. Simultaneously, our mind instantly races with all the limiting thoughts and beliefs about how it's not possible for us to achieve that desire. Be aware of what happens in your mind and body as you go through this process.

Looking at your list of desires and purpose from the previous chapter, consider one desire at a time and ask yourself the following two questions:

How do I feel about manifesting this?
What's preventing me from manifesting this?

Use your journal to write down whatever comes up. These could be thoughts, beliefs, fears, or other emotions.

As soon as you have a list of fears, emotions, thoughts, and beliefs, choose the ones that feel stronger and most dominant and ask yourself "why" five times. Asking yourself *why* you fear or believe something five times will allow you to get to the core limiting beliefs behind them.

Fears and limiting beliefs tend to be layered, in the sense that we have core beliefs such as "I'm not a good person" that create minor limiting beliefs such as "I can't do this." By asking *why* five times, we go down the layers until we reach the core belief/s that created the minor ones. When you work on identifying the core beliefs rather than just the minor ones you hit two birds with one stone, thus speeding up the healing process.

In the next chapters, you'll learn cognitive and energetic practices for processing and releasing your core limiting beliefs.

———————⋙⟨⟩⋘———————

17

RELEASE YOUR LIMITING BELIEFS COGNITIVELY

Having followed the Five Whys exercise in the previous chapter, you'll have ended up with a series of core beliefs that currently prevent you from manifesting your desires and purpose. These limiting beliefs will likely include personal pronouns, such as "*I* am not good enough," "*I* am not talented," "People like *me* don't succeed," and "*I* can't do it by *myself*." These core beliefs don't represent who you are, but instead who you have learned you are as a result of various experiences and circumstances in your life.

As with your emotions, these core beliefs are also like buckets that hold a series of past memories that helped create and strengthen your false identity imprints. In the same way that you used IEMT to identify and desensitize past memories creating negative emotions, you can also do so with your core beliefs. Rather than using the eye movement pattern you used in Chapter 12, we'll use a slightly different pattern for this exercise.

How to Release Limiting Beliefs with IEMT

To demonstrate the process, let's consider the limiting belief of "*I* am not talented." In this case, the pronoun used is the *I*, and *I* believes that they are not talented. To identify the series of memories and life circumstances that led to that belief, you're going to ask *I* a series of questions. It's important not to overthink these questions, but to let the answers come up naturally. Your body and being know the answers, and asking the questions will prompt the answers.

With the core belief in mind, ask yourself the following:

When you think of I, where is I?

As soon as you ask this, notice where you feel *I* is. It may be somewhere within your body, outside of your body, or even somewhere in the past. There are no right or wrong answers to this question, so let yourself take you where *I* is.

Then, ask yourself the following:

How old is I there?

Don't overthink this question, and go with the first age from your past that comes to mind.

Finally, continue with a third question:

What's happening around x-years-old I there?

This is the part when you'll cognitively access a specific life experience, circumstance, or memory that has contributed to the creation of your core limiting belief. Allow the details of this experience to come up. If what comes up is a specific memory with a negative emotion attached to it, go back to Chapter 12 and use the IEMT process to transmute negative emotions. If what comes up is a general life circumstance without a specific memory attached to it, continue with the eye-movement pattern in the next step.

Eye-Movement Pattern

With your head aligned straight ahead and only moving your eyes, draw the infinity sign on the next page with your eyes. It's important to go all the way to the edges of where your eyes can stretch, so that you feel a gentle pull of the eye muscles. Move your eyes for 15 seconds in one direction and then 15 seconds in the opposite direction. This eye movement pattern helps rewire your perception of these experiences, taking away their negative identity imprint, thus helping release your core belief.

Once you've done the eye practice (whether you used the emotional or identity eye-movement process), ask yourself the initial three questions:

How old is I now?

Where is I?

What's happening around x-years-old I there?

The usual trajectory of this process is that you start at a younger age and then progressively move forward to the present moment, and then possibly to the future. Often, once you've reached the present moment or a future point in time, you'll end up having a more positive outlook on yourself, your desires, and your purpose. Once you've reached this point, go back to the original core limiting belief and ask yourself whether it's still true for you. It most probably won't be! By this point, you'll have identified the majority of the past identity imprints that created this core belief and desensitized them, so that they no longer uphold the limiting belief.

Do this process with all your core limiting beliefs until you've identified and released them fully. When you're done, proceed with releasing them energetically, too; more on this in the next chapter.

Mark's Journey to Healthy Relationships

Mark arrived at our sessions after enduring a series of toxic relationships and heartbreaks. He yearned for a fulfilling partnership with a like-minded individual, but found himself repeatedly attracting unavailable men into his life. Mark's journey was plagued by a core limiting belief that whispered, "I'm not worthy of love," continuously undermining his dating experiences. Our exploration led us to untangle the roots of his fears and limiting beliefs, revealing a profound connection to his childhood experiences.

Through the IEMT process, we embarked on a transformative journey to uncover the source of Mark's struggles. It became clear that his deep-seated belief of unworthiness originated from never receiving sufficient love and attention from his parents during his formative years. This upbringing forged an anxious attachment style within Mark, leading to neediness and co-dependency in his relationships. Desperate for love, he unknowingly pushed his partners away, perpetuating a cycle of disappointment.

With each IEMT session, we gently peeled back the layers of Mark's past, unveiling and releasing the traumatic memories that had held him captive. Through this healing process, he began to rebuild his relationship with his parents, fostering understanding, forgiveness, and, ultimately, self-acceptance. As the wounds of the past started to heal, Mark's perception of his own worthiness of love shifted, paving the way for transformative change.

Several months after our sessions, I received a message from Mark, overflowing with newfound confidence and gratitude. While he was still single, he was now approaching the dating experience with a fresh perspective, no longer burdened by the weight of neediness and co-dependency. Mark had learned to honour himself, to not attach too soon and to allow relationships to unfold organically. He discovered the power of self-love and the importance of setting healthy boundaries, realizing that the right person would come into his life when the time was right.

18

RELEASE YOUR LIMITING BELIEFS ENERGETICALLY

Amistake people make when doing the inner work is that they solely focus on cognitive or emotional processes, and don't address the energetic component behind their limiting beliefs. When we adopt a limiting belief, it leaves an energetic imprint within our energy field. When I scan people's energy as part of my psychic clearing sessions, I clairvoyantly see these limiting beliefs stored as energy blocks within their chakras, energy cords connected to the collective frequency of the limiting beliefs, and etheric blockages within the mental layer of their aura.

Unless we identify and release the energetic imprints of our limiting beliefs, there is a good chance that they'll eventually resurface. This is because limiting beliefs manifest energetically first, before they escalate into thoughts, beliefs, and emotions. To understand how this works, think of your limiting beliefs as weeds. The energetic imprints of your limiting beliefs are the roots of the weeds, while their cognitive and emotional expression are the stalks and leaves. When we do the cognitive and emotional work we trim the weeds, but unless we uproot them they'll eventually grow back.

How to Identify the Energetic Imprint of Your Limiting Beliefs

In the following meditation, you'll get to identify the energetic imprints of your limiting beliefs, and use energetic processes to release them fully.

Step 1—Turn On Your 360-Degree Vision

Having centred and grounded yourself, bring your attention to your third-eye chakra. Your third-eye chakra is the control centre of your intuition and inner vision, and you can visualize it as a ball of purple light in the centre of your head, in-between your eyebrows.

Then turn on your 360-degree inner vision. Although your physical eyes can only see what's right in front of you and to your periphery, your third eye can observe in all directions at the same time.

To do this, with your eyes closed use your inner vision to perceive what's right in front of you. Let your imagination guide the way, and perceive what's in the physical, three-dimensional space in front of you, as well as what's in the non-physical dimensions parallel to it. After a few breaths, expand your inner vision to perceive what's to your right and left, while maintaining your perception of what's in front of you. Continue expanding your vision to perceive what's above, below, and behind you, until you can perceive in all directions at the same time.

Step 2—Scan Your Energy Field

With your 360-degree vision turned on, set an intention to identify the energetic imprints of your limiting beliefs. Then, scan your body and aura from top to bottom, noticing where you feel drawn to go. You may visually see darker energy, etheric cobwebs, or energetic mucus in different parts of your chakras, body, and aura. Trust whatever comes through and don't second-guess your intuition. Your ego will want to come in to try to sabotage your findings, so be aware of it and don't let it get in the way.

As you identify each blockage, you may get a sense of what limiting belief it relates to. You may also identify limiting beliefs you hadn't identified cognitively. Trust the process, and, after you've scanned your body and identified everything, proceed with the next step.

Step 3—Clear the Energy of Your Limiting Beliefs

There are many cleansing tools, processes, and spirit guides you can work with to clear the energy of your limiting beliefs. See my book *Protect Your Light*, or use a process you're familiar with. For the purpose of this exercise, we'll use the energy vacuuming technique.

With your eyes still closed, visualize an energetic vacuum cleaner that has the ability to suck away the energy of your limiting beliefs. You may call upon one of your spirit guides to support you in this process. With intention, turn the energetic vacuum cleaner on and direct it to the various parts of your energy field, removing and transmuting each and every limiting belief you've identified previously.

Step 4—Seal Your Energy Field

Having cleared the energy of your limiting beliefs, you need to heal the energetic scarring, wounds, and holes that removing the limiting beliefs has created in your energy field. Clearing energetic attachments is similar to undergoing surgery, in the sense that once you've been operated on the doctors need to sew the wounds up. If you skip this step, you run the risk of having the energetic blockages returning or going through a rough purging and healing crisis after the clearing.

To seal your energy call upon the emerald-green ray, a Universal healing frequency of light that will seep through the scars of your energy field to mend and heal them. Visualize yourself surrounded by a healing cocoon of emerald-green light for a few minutes, or until you feel complete.

Once you're done with the process, gradually bring some movement into your body and come out of the meditation.

For a few hours to a week after clearing your energy, you may experience purging symptoms or go through a healing crisis. Having released the energy of your limiting beliefs and adjusted your energy field, your body and being will go ahead and release any remaining toxins related to them. You may experience this as moodiness, increased negative thoughts, or even flu-like symptoms such as coughing and a runny nose. This is all part of the process, so make sure to support yourself with physical movement, lots of water, and healthy food.

Jenna's Transformation into a Successful Spiritual Artist

Jenna was a talented artist with a deep passion for capturing people's energy through painting. She longed to turn her artistic endeavours into a thriving business, but she was held back by a web of fears and limiting beliefs. Thoughts such as "I'm not good enough," "Nobody will like my work," and "It's been done before" constantly played in her mind, hindering her from pursuing her dreams.

Determined to overcome these barriers, Jenna delved into various cognitive practices like EFT tapping, journaling, and CBT. Although these techniques provided some relief, she still found herself trapped by the weight of her fears.

I assisted Jenna in recognizing and releasing the energetic attachments associated with her fears and limiting beliefs. These attachments were entangled within the mental layer of her aura, perpetually connected to the collective frequency of these self-imposed restrictions. Through a transformative healing session, we untangled these cords, liberating Jenna from the grip of her doubts.

Following the session, Jenna experienced a profound breakthrough. With her mind no longer entangled in self-doubt, she gained clarity about how she could position and market her paintings in a way that truly resonated with her desired audience. Although remnants of fear and resistance still lingered within her, they no longer held the same power over her aspirations.

And so, Jenna launched her business, embodying the essence of a successful spiritual artist. Today, she stands as a shining example of how combining cognitive practices and energy healing can transform and move one's life forward toward a desired outcome.

19

ACTUALIZE THE CHANGE

A big mistake people make when doing the inner work is not backing it up with action. Mental transmutation isn't just about completing a cognitive process or releasing energy attachments; in truth, that's just the beginning of it. Having worked through your limiting beliefs using the previous two processes, you will have changed your mental, emotional, and energetic outlook significantly. However, unless you take action towards actualizing these changes, your limiting beliefs may resurface.

During or soon after the healing crisis period, the Universe will likely bring into your life opportunities to help you solidify your inner transformation. These opportunities may come as conversations you're prompted to have with people, career shifts and changes, moving house, taking trips, getting into or ending relationships, etc. It's important to notice these opportunities when they show up, and then have the courage to follow through with them.

Often, the ego, in its final attempt to sabotage our growth, will use this time to create obstacles or excuses to making these changes. When opportunities for change come up, you may find yourself thinking, "I've already worked on this issue," or "I've released this energetically; I don't need to do something more about it." When these thoughts come up, remind yourself that cognitive and energy work are just the first steps to the healing journey. To complete the process, you eed to take physical and palpable action steps forward.

To do so, a few days after the cognitive and energy release use the following journal prompts to reflect on your growth:

▷ *What action steps do I feel guided to take to embrace my new-found self?*

▷ *What areas of my life do I need to make changes in, so that they reflect my new beliefs?*

▷ *What conversations do I need to have?*

▷ *What relationship issues do I need to address?*

▷ *What do I need to release?*

▷ *How does the new me think, feel, and show up in the world?*

Once you've journaled and have come up with an action plan, make sure to follow through with it on a daily basis, and for as long as it takes for you to complete the process.

Moving forward, keep these questions in mind when you're doing any form of mental transmutation, whether it's cognitive or energetic, so you can keep releasing your limiting beliefs and supporting the manifestation process.

How I Healed Self-Doubt and Manifested a Fulfilling Sex Life

During the summer of 2020, I underwent a profound healing journey. It all began when I faced romantic and sexual rejections from men I was interested in, triggering deep-seated self-doubts and limiting beliefs that had haunted me since childhood. My mind became flooded with the cruel words and names my bullies had hurled at me for years: "you're ugly," "you're fat," "nobody loves you," "what a freak!"

Determined to finally overcome these suffocating beliefs, I embarked on a path of cognitive and energetic healing. I dedicated myself to healing my inner child, reshaping my perception of myself, and cultivating a positive self-image.

I predominantly employed techniques such as IEMT, EFT tapping, and energy healing practices to transform my old identity and embrace a new version of myself. By the time I finished, I felt like an entirely renewed person.

However, I made the mistake of becoming complacent about my breakthrough, and failed to take action to actualize my newfound state of being. Instead of getting out there and actualizing my inner change with real, physical experiences, I settled for merely acknowledging its occurrence. But the Universe had different plans in store for me.

When I finally re-entered the dating scene months later, I found myself slipping back into some of the same limiting beliefs I had worked so hard to let go of. Fortunately, I had undergone enough healing to confront and overcome these patterns, and so could prevent them from sabotaging my experiences. From that moment on, I made a commitment to, following my healing journeys, immediately push myself beyond my comfort zone, and actualize my inner changes.

Although the results didn't manifest instantly, and I still often find myself revisiting certain doubts and limiting beliefs (as we all know, the healing journey is an ongoing process), each encounter with them weakens their grip on me, making them more manageable. As a result, the traumas of my childhood no longer hold me back, and I am now able to enjoy a healthy and fulfilling sex life.

20

CREATE NEW, SUPPORTIVE BELIEFS

Having identified and transmuted your limiting beliefs that are blocking the manifestation of your desires, both cognitively and energetically, the next step in the process of mental transmutation is to replace your limiting beliefs with new and supportive ones. Unless you create these new beliefs, you may be naturally inclined to revert to the old, limiting beliefs simply because you're more familiar with them.

Instead, when you go ahead and come up with new beliefs, you give your mind and energy something new to focus on and nurture. This way, you slow down the mental and energetic momentum of the old beliefs and start building a new, positive momentum of the supportive beliefs. Eventually, once you've fully taken them on and nurtured their energy, they'll become part of your energetic make-up in the same way the previous beliefs were, and you won't have to try to believe them. They'll simply be part of your new reality.

How to Create New Beliefs

Follow the process below to create new, supportive beliefs for your life and fill them with energy.

Step 1—Craft Your New Beliefs

The first step towards coming up with new beliefs that support the manifestation of your desires is to put them into words. To do so, you need to go back to the list of limiting beliefs you came up with in Chapter 16, and consciously turn them round, into positive beliefs.

When doing so, it's important that your new beliefs are both positive and believable. Therefore, they should be positive enough that they're not limiting your manifestation efforts, but also believable, so that believing them doesn't seem impossible. If your positive beliefs are positive but feel impossible, it'll likely be harder for you to take them on, or at the least it'll take more time for you to do so.

As a result, it's a good idea to use phrases such as, *"I'm in the process of . . .," "I'm becoming more . . .," "I'm gradually . . .,"* or *"I'm open to . . ."* These phrases refer to the process of change rather than stating something absolute, and thus instantly feel more believable, while also being positive.

For example:

"I'm not worthy of success" could be "I'm feeling more worthy of success each day."

"I need more training before I'm able to do this" could be rephrased more positively as "I'm becoming more and more equipped to accomplish this every day."

"I'm not good enough to write a book" could turn into "I'm in the process of becoming a better writer."

Eventually, as you get comfortable with these new beliefs, you can change them into more absolute beliefs, because you will be in a better cognitive and emotional position to accept them.

Step 2—Affirm Your New Beliefs

Once you've phrased your new beliefs, you then need to believe them. In the same way as you've released your negative beliefs in both cognitive and energetic ways, you can work on creating new, supportive beliefs.

My favourite cognitive process for nurturing new beliefs is using affirmations. Affirmations are simply statements you make about yourself. You make them all day every day when talking to others about yourself, your beliefs, and your perception of the world. Making affirmations involves consciously speaking them out loud in an effort to embody them and make them part of your new belief system.

Made popular by Louise Hay in her bestselling book *You Can Heal Your Life*, positive affirmations have become a popular tool for changing our beliefs and manifesting our desires. The process involves writing down a list of positive affirmations of the new beliefs you want to adopt, and repeating them out loud, usually while looking at yourself in the mirror. Looking in the mirror has the added benefit of helping you access any possible limiting beliefs that may still prevent you from believing the new ones, so that you can identify and release them. As Louise Hay puts it in her book *Mirror Work*, "the mirror reflects back to you the feelings you have about yourself. It makes you immediately aware of where you are resisting and where you are open and flowing."

To further improve their efficacy, I like to speak out my positive affirmations while tapping and looking at myself in the mirror. Tapping or Emotional Freedom Technique (EFT) is an energy psychology modality that involves tapping on different parts of your body while repeating certain statements. Although it's traditionally associated with releasing negative emotions, it can also be used to amplify positive ones. Thus, when combining your positive affirmations with tapping, you get the added benefit of amplifying the positive emotions elicited by your affirmations.

Ideally, do your positive affirmations daily for at least 30 days, or for as long as you need, to fully embody your newfound beliefs. Every few weeks, you can revisit your list of affirmations and update them with a new set of beliefs to keep upgrading your belief system.

Step 3—Connect to the Energy of Your New Beliefs

The final step in the process of creating new beliefs is to embody their energy. In Chapter 18, you learned to identify and release the energetic attachment of your negative beliefs from within your energy field. In this step, you'll reverse the process and instead instil the energy of the new beliefs in your energy.

Each belief, whether positive or negative, exists as a collective frequency in the ether of the Universe. Think of these collective frequencies as vibrational clouds that you can establish relationships with. In a meditative state, let your consciousness search the Universe to identify the collective energy of your new beliefs.

With your positive beliefs in mind, visualize yourself as a vibrational magnet attracting their collective energy to you. Let energetic cords extend from your body and hook into their collective frequencies, creating a permanent connection to them.

As soon as you've done so, you'll start receiving thoughts, emotions, and impulses, which will help you embody them. Bask in this state for a while, until you feel connected to the energy of your new beliefs. When the process feels complete, slowly bring some movement into your body and come out of the meditation.

How Positive Affirmations Saved My Life

At the age of 15 I found myself in tears on the floor of my room, clutching a handful of pills, ready to surrender my life. It was the culmination of two years filled with self-loathing and relentless attempts to cure myself of what I believed was the affliction of homosexuality.

But in that darkest hour, a profound realization washed over me like a divine whisper. A voice from within urged me to release the shackles of others' opinions and embrace a radical love and acceptance for myself. I had no roadmap to guide me, but I trusted that the voice that had saved me would illuminate my path.

Soon after that epiphany, I embarked on a spiritual journey of healing and personal transformation. Tools, books, and wise spiritual mentors seemed to materialize at every turn, offering me methods to mend the wounds I had inflicted upon myself.

Among the first luminaries to enter my life was Louise Hay, a teacher who would leave an indelible mark on my journey. I vividly recall stumbling upon her timeless explanation of the power of positive affirmations. In *You Can Heal Your Life* (mentioned earlier), Louise beautifully articulated that affirmations are like seeds—planted through creation, nurtured by repetition, and blossoming into flowers that transform our lives.

Though I couldn't fully comprehend the mechanism at work, I sensed its inherent truth and resolved to give it a chance. The very next day, I eagerly purchased Louise's affirmations CD, *101 Power Thoughts*. From the moment I pressed play, I was captivated.

For an entire year, I faithfully listened to that hour-long recording every day without fail. It became the soundtrack of my life, accompanying me during commutes, echoing through my workplace, and gently lulling me to sleep each night. I even inscribed my favourite affirmations on Post-it notes all across the walls of my home, the bathroom mirror, my computer screen, and even the windscreen of my car. That CD became my obsession and, to this day, if you were to play any part of the recording I could tell you what comes next.

After a year of unwavering dedication, something extraordinary began to occur. The affirmations had taken root so deeply in my subconscious that they started to manifest in my reality. What was once an elusive dream—believing I was in the right place, at the right time, doing the right thing—now felt like a natural truth. The seemingly unattainable affirmation of "I love and accept myself" became a simple, genuine expression of my being.

Of course, the practice of affirmations had brought forth fears, frustrations, and resentments that I diligently worked to heal and release. Yet, having Louise's soothing voice affirming that "Everything unfolds at the perfect time when I'm ready" made the journey of healing so much gentler than I could've ever imagined.

Reflecting upon my life's journey thus far, considering the depths from which I emerged and the distance I have travelled, I can wholeheartedly say that Louise Hay's work not only altered the course of my life, but it also saved me. The story I have just shared is merely a fraction of the profound impact Louise's teachings have had on my healing and growth over the years. Whenever I lose my way, I return to that sacred recording that ignited it all, to remind myself that "Life is really simple" and that "All is well."

STEP 4

Nurture the Energy of Your Desires

21

PLANT YOUR DESIRES IN YOUR ENERGY FIELD

So far in the five-step manifestation process, you've raised your vibration, clarified your desires, released limiting beliefs, and created new, supportive ones. The fourth step of the process is to nurture the energy of your desires. This step is tied to the laws of vibration and mentalism.

The law of vibration explains that to manifest your desires you need to consistently match your vibrational frequency to the frequency of your desires. The majority of the manifestation processes focus on this step, and include processes such as visualization, vision boards, and scripting, to help you raise your vibration to the frequency of achieving your desires. While these are all effective processes, and ones I do use in my manifestation practice, I also use energy-based processes that amplify my vibrational frequency in relation to specific desires, thus speeding up their manifestation.

The law of mentalism explains that manifestation takes place when the creator becomes involved in, or wrapped up with, the energy of their desire, a process called involution or outpouring. In this process, the creator directs energy into the mental image of their creation until it gathers up enough energetic momentum that it expresses in a physical way. Although this process happens naturally all day every day as we live life, we can use it in a more conscious way when manifesting specific desires.

Combining the laws of vibration and mentalism, by becoming wrapped up with our desires, and thus directing energy to them, we match our vibrational frequency to the specific frequency of our desires. The usual manifestation processes such as scripting and vision boards help us do that in a physical way, but energy processes work on a more subtle level to alchemize the manifestation of our desires.

How to Plant Your Desires in Your Energy Field

Follow the three steps below to plant your desires in your energy field.

Step 1—Get to Know the Energy of Your Desires

Since you already have a mental image or intention of what your specific desires are, the next step is to become *involved in* their creation by directing energy towards them, and thus matching your vibration to their vibration. To understand how this works in a more visual way, think of your desires as orbs of energy. In the same way that your physical body, and all physical things around you, have an energetic presence, what's known as the aura or energy field, so do your desires. When you become aware and familiar of your desires' energy fields, you can invite them into your presence, connect with them, infuse them with your energy, and make them your own.

To do this, while in a meditative state invite the energy of your desires to enter your energy field. You can say something along the lines of, "I call upon the energy of my desires to come into my presence." Once you set out your intention, you'll feel your desires lighting up as orbs of energy around you. If they happen to show up further away from you, use your intention to draw them closer.

Starting with one desire at a time, spend some time observing and getting to know them energetically. Specifically, notice their colour, texture, density, the sound they make, the taste they may have, the way they feel, and the kind of thoughts that come to mind when you perceive them. This process will allow you to understand your desires on an energetic level, so you can access and mould their energy more easily.

Step 2—Cord Your Desires in Your Energy Field

Having got to know the energy of your desires, the next step is to cord them in your energy field. This involves visualizing an energetic cord extending from the energy of each desire and connecting to your energetic body, usually to one or more of your chakras. To do this, simply set the intention to cord your desires to you, and visualize the cords extending and attaching to you.

Rather than attaching them to specific chakras, I always let my desires choose what chakra or other part of my body they want to make a connection with, and I simply observe and remember their choice.

Step 3—Match Your Frequency to the Frequency of Your Desires

Once you've attached your desires to you, focus on the energetic exchange that will naturally start to take place. Your energetic connection allows energy to flow both ways, so that you can infuse your desires with specific thoughts, images, and energy, and your desires can infuse their own energetic communication to you, through the cord. Bask in this position for a while and notice this energetic exchange take place.

To amplify this process, consciously invite the energy of your desires into your own energy. Feel the vibrational frequency of each desire flow through the energetic cord and into your energy field, tuning you to that frequency too. Imagine these energies as vibrational vitamins that seep through every pore of your being and tune you to the frequency of your desires. While this energetic transmission takes place you will likely feel your vibration changing; it's important to keep your body relaxed and breathe deeply, to allow this process to take place naturally.

As you tune your frequency to the frequency of your desires, you may also start getting downloads of action steps that you can take to bring your desires to life. Keep an eye out for these downloads and make a note of them after the meditation.

When this transmission feels complete, slowly bring some movement into your hands and shoulders and come out of the meditation. Be sure to have your journal nearby so you can take notes of your desires' energetic location, the chakras they're connected to, and any ideas and action steps that came up.

The Importance of Planting Your Desires in Your Energy Field

In her book *Big Magic*, Elizabeth Gilbert supports the notion that ideas, and consequently desires, are intelligent living entities with the singular purpose of manifesting themselves:

"I believe that our planet is inhabited not only by animals and plants and bacteria and viruses, but also by ideas . . . Ideas are a disembodied, energetic life-form . . . Ideas spend eternity swirling around us, searching for available and willing human partners . . . When an idea thinks it has found somebody—say, you—who might be able to bring it into the world, the idea will pay you a visit. It will try to get your attention . . . The idea will try to wave you down (perhaps for a few moments; perhaps for a few months; perhaps even for a few years), but when it finally realizes that you're oblivious to its message, it will move on to someone else."

Elizabeth's theory aligns with the law of mentalism, which elucidates the relationship between the energetic and physical aspects of our desires. It also sheds light on the repercussions of failing to plant our desires in our energy field. Unless we actively engage with the energy of our desires by planting them and taking concrete steps to manifest them, they will eventually seek out new hosts.

There have been countless occasions in the past when I conceived ideas for new books and online courses, only to be hindered by other commitments. Eventually, I would discover that someone else had beaten me to the punch. Recognizing that desires are living entities, I consciously developed the habit of planting them in my energy field and nurturing my connection to them on a daily basis. Consequently, I keep these desires engaged until the time comes for me to dedicate the necessary time and energy.

However, it is important to acknowledge that I cannot keep them confined within my energy field indefinitely. If left unmanifested, they will inevitably find a way to escape, which fuels my drive to bring them to life. At present, I have my two next book title ideas firmly planted within my energy field. To ensure their continued engagement and prevent their departure, I activate their energy using the practices outlined in subsequent chapters, while also engaging in daily research.

22

RAISE THE VIBRATION OF
YOUR DESIRES

Planting your desires in your energy field is a powerful way to nurture, and align to, their vibrational frequency. This energetic process will also help support and amplify the effectiveness of your other manifestation processes, such as journaling, visualization, positive affirmations, etc.

In this and the next three chapters, I'll teach you four additional, advanced energetic processes that you can use to further nurture and amplify your energetic connection to your desires. The first process has to do with connecting the energy of your desires to the collective frequency of emotional states, to speed up their manifestation.

If your desire has to do with manifesting your ideal partner, you can connect the energy of this desire to the emotional frequency of love or joy. The collective frequency of an emotion holds the totality of every thought, emotion, belief, or experience relating to that emotion that has ever been thought, felt, and experienced, by everything and everyone across time and space.

For example, the collective frequency of love holds the totality of every loving thought, emotion, belief, or experience that has ever existed. By tuning to that frequency, you feed off that energy, which raises the frequency of your desire and supports its manifestation.

How to Raise the Vibration of Your Desires

Follow these steps to raise the vibration of your desires by connecting them to emotional frequencies:

Step 1—Choose the Frequencies to Connect To

Before you connect your desires to specific frequencies, you first have to choose the right frequencies for each desire. To do so, start by bringing up the list with the desires you've already planted into your energy field. Going through each desire, consider what emotional states would benefit each desire and help its manifestation.

To find the right emotions, ask yourself, "How would having this desire make me feel?," and write down the emotions that come to mind. Then, keep asking yourself, "How do these emotions feel?," and notice what similar-feeling emotions come up. These questions will eventually lead you to the emotional signature of each desire, therefore, the exact emotion or emotions describing how the manifestation of each desire will make you feel. Ideally, choose a maximum of three emotions for each desire.

Step 2—Hook Your Desires to Your Chosen Frequencies

Having chosen the best emotional frequencies for your desires, go into a meditative state and bring up the energies of your desires within your energy field. With the intention to connect them to your chosen collective frequencies, visualize energetic cords extending from the centre of each desire's energy, reaching out to the Universe and finding the collective frequencies of your chosen emotions, and hooking into them.

As soon as you hook into the collective frequencies, you'll feel a transmission of energy from the collective frequency to your desire's energy, and finally to your own energy. This will be a transmission of thoughts, emotions, energy, and impulses, all focused around bringing your desires to life. This transmission will raise the vibrational frequency of both your desires and yourself, and ultimately speed up the manifestation process. Set the intention that your desires stay hooked into these frequencies for as long as it's needed for them to manifest.

Step 3—Bask in the Energy and Receive

Before you come out of meditation, make sure to bask in the energy of these connections for at least ten minutes. During this time, breathe deeply and allow your desires and your being to charge up on the collective energy of your chosen emotions. Be mindful of the thoughts, ideas, and impulses around ways in which you can take action towards the manifestation of your desires, and make a note of them in your journal after the meditation.

When the process feels complete, gradually bring some movement into your body and come out of the meditation.

How I Manifested This Book—Part One

The way I manifested the publication of this book attests to the effectiveness of the process.

When I presented *Ancient Manifestation Secrets* (*AMS*) to my publisher at the time, they suggested that the book was too advanced for publication and asked me to present a different book idea with the hope of publishing *AMS* afterward. I went with their suggestion, however, I wasn't ready to give up. I knew that I was guided to write *AMS* for a reason and that I had to find a publisher who believed in it as much as I did and was ready to move forward without hesitation.

By infusing the energy of this book into my field, I identified and connected with the emotional frequencies needed for its manifestation, strengthening that connection daily for two years. It would have been easy to take my publisher's word for granted and abandon the project. However, consistently activating the frequency of its manifestation kept me focused and motivated. With trust in the Universe's laws, I knew the book would manifest when the timing was right, as long as I cooperated. Activating the emotional frequency of its manifestation helped me achieve this.

———❦———

23

CONNECT WITH HELPFUL PEOPLE

A side from hooking your desires to emotional frequencies, you can also energetically connect with helpful people, businesses, and organizations, that will assist with their manifestation. As explained in Chapter 7, manifestation is a collaborative process that involves the cooperation of various factors to bring a desire into creation—what Abraham-Hicks refer to as cooperative components.

One category of such cooperative components is people willing to support you on your journey, either knowingly or unknowingly. A lot of the literature on manifestation makes us feel that manifesting something is solely up to us and our vibrational frequency. Whereas this is true to a great degree, as I explained in Chapter 7 there are many different components that contribute to manifestation, our vibration being just one of them.

By reaching out to energetically connect with people who can support us on our journey, we shift our mindset from manifestation egotism to collaboration. This eases the pressure and responsibility to manifest everything ourselves, and instead allows us to be one of the many cooperative components that work together to bring our desires to life.

It's important to stress that energetically connecting with people who can support us on our journey isn't about manipulating them to do so. Instead of forcefully making energetic connections to them, we reach out energetically and allow the people who wish to support us anyway to make a connection with us and our desires.

These connections take place on a spiritual and energetic level; thus, we may not necessarily know the people we're connecting with, or ever get to meet them in real life. Instead, we make spiritual agreements to support one another through choices and action steps that play a part in manifesting our desires and life purpose.

The law of cause and effect states that all manifestations are merely effects of previous causes, meaning that behind every manifestation there have been a myriad of causes that led to their expression. From this perspective, by connecting with helpful people we consciously reach out to orchestrate a series of causes that will contribute to, and speed up, the effects of our desires manifesting.

How to Connect Your Desires to Helpful People

Follow these steps to consciously connect your desires with helpful people, businesses, and organizations who might be able to support their manifestation:

Step 1—Extend Energetic Filaments Out in the World

Once you are in a meditative state, visualize the energy of your desires within your energy field. Spend some time reacquainting yourself with them and feeling the transmission of energy between you.

Once you've done so, visualize hundreds of thin energetic filaments extending out from each desire's energy and spreading around the world. Think of these filaments as energetic scouts that search for supportive people, businesses, and organizations that can support you in manifesting your desires. These are filaments instead of cords because you don't want all of them to hook into the people and businesses they connect with. Instead, these filaments will make an initial contact to gauge the degree to which they are able and willing to support you in manifesting your desires.

Spend a few minutes in this state, and let the energetic filaments search around the world and find the right group of people to connect with.

Step 2—Make Energetic Connections with Willing Hosts

Once the filaments have found cooperative hosts, they'll then make a more permanent connection to them and become cords. Rather than trying to control this process, just let it happen naturally. Simply, be aware of the filaments and notice the ones retreating and fading away, and the ones that stick and start getting thicker.

Once the filaments start getting thicker and turning into cords, consciously facilitate an energetic flow from you to your desires' orbs, and from there to the hosts that you've connected to. You'll also likely feel an energetic exchange, as the hosts send energy back to you, too. You don't need to spend time identifying who these hosts are, but simply trust that they're people, businesses, and organizations that will actively help you manifest your desires.

Eventually, all the filaments that couldn't make a connection will fade away and you'll be left with a selection of cords connecting your desires to helpful people as envisioned. Spend some time basking in this state and feeling the energetic exchange taking place, and, when the process feels complete, bring some movement into your body and come out of the meditation.

How I Manifested This Book—Part Two

Over the many years I've practised conscious manifestation I've noticed that, when the timing is ripe for manifestation, things escalate rapidly! This was precisely the case with the manifestation of *Ancient Manifestation Secrets*. Sabine, the editor at Findhorn Press, and I had been discussing the book for several months, but arranging a meeting to finalize the details seemed elusive. Taking it as a sign from the Universe that other factors were in play, I decided to let go and trust that everything would unfold at the right time.

Simultaneously, I had already established multiple energetic cords with supportive people and entities, including Findhorn Press. I consistently activated and nurtured these connections for months.

One afternoon, while meditating, I received a clear psychic hit to email Sabine about the book. It was an unmistakable and urgent download that demanded immediate action. After concluding my meditation, I promptly wrote to her and, incredibly, within ten minutes she responded, asking if we could have a Zoom meeting right then and there. The Universe had orchestrated everything perfectly; I had a last-minute session cancellation that allowed me to jump on the call right away.

The meeting went remarkably well. We reached an agreement on the terms and Sabine offered me a book deal! As if that wasn't enough, a week later, on July 2023, just after completing my full moon manifestation ritual, during which I specifically activated the book's energy, I received the official offer via email.

Throughout the months of communication, there were several instances where I could have given up on my desire. Usually, when I pitch books or other projects, I send publishers one or two emails, and often give up if I don't receive a prompt reply. However, the fact that the energetic filaments I'd sent out to Findhorn Press persisted and evolved into lasting cords reassured me that there was genuine interest. By continuously keeping those connections activated, I collaboratively worked with the Universe to bring this book to life, in perfect alignment with the destined timing.

—————⋐?⋑—————

24

RECEIVE HELP FROM ELEMENTAL AND SPIRITUAL BEINGS

The third process for amplifying the manifestation power of your desires is to connect with elemental beings and spirit guides that will aid their manifestation.

The law of correspondence explains that there's fluidity between the physical, mental, and spiritual planes. Therefore, by raising our vibration we have the opportunity to connect, communicate with, and receive help from the physical or spiritual beings in each plane. In this process, you'll get to consciously reach out to make energetic connection with such beings so that you can amplify your attraction power and speed up the manifestation of your desires.

How to Connect Your Desires to Elemental and Spiritual Beings

Follow these steps to connect your desires to elemental and spiritual beings that can help with their manifestation:

Step 1—Tune In to the Frequency of Your Desires

Before you connect your desires to cooperative components that can aid their manifestation, take some time to meditate and reconnect with them once more.

While in meditation, bring up the visual or emotional image of the energetic orbs you've planted in your energy field. Remind yourself of their energetic make-up and characteristics, the chakras they're connected to, and the emotions you've hooked them into.

It's important to re-familiarize yourself with the work you've done so far, so that you can connect your desires to the spirit guides that are most in tune with them. Spend some time in this state, feeling the energetic exchange between you and your desires, as well as allowing the transmission of energy between the emotional frequencies you connected them with.

Step 2—Connect to the Mental and Spiritual Planes

As explained in Chapter 3, the elemental beings in the mental plane of existence, as well as the various angels, gods and goddesses, and other spiritual beings in the spiritual plane of existence, can all help you manifest your desires. In this step of the process, you'll raise your vibration to connect to both realms, so that you can easily connect with the beings that wish to support your manifestation journey.

To connect with the elemental beings within the mental plane of existence, extend four cords of attachment from your root chakra and connect to the collective frequency of the four physical elements—earth, air, fire, and water. While connecting to each element, allow your mind and body to energetically merge with the energy of each element. To do so, feel how it would feel to be each element, and fill your mind with images of it. For example, while cording yourself to the element of water, feel how it would feel to be water, and let your mind picture rivers, lakes, and the ocean. As you connect with each element, allow the energy of the elements and their elementals to flow through these cords and into your body.

To connect with the spiritual beings within the spiritual plane of existence, extend an energetic cord from your crown chakra and let it reach up to the ether and connect with the crystalline palace you connected with in Chapter 14. Rather than journey up through the cord to the palace, simply let the energy of Source flow down through the cord and saturate your body.

By infusing your being with energy from both the elemental and spiritual realms, you instantly gain access to the elemental and spiritual beings that inhabit each realm. Spend some time basking in this state of connectedness, and become aware of how your vibrational frequency shifts as a result.

Step 3—Invite Elemental and Spiritual Beings to Support You

After some time connecting with the frequency of spirit and the elements, you may start sensing various elemental and spiritual beings making contact with you. Mentally or out loud, set your intention that you want to connect with elemental and spiritual beings that are willing and able to support you in manifesting your desires.

If you're already familiar and in contact with such beings, it'll be easier for you to sense their presence and communicate with them. Spend some time noticing who shows up and what desires they're most interested in supporting you with.

If you don't have experience working with the elementals and other spirit guides and need some guidance, here's a list of popular guides that you may encounter.

Elemental Beings

From a spiritual perspective, the Earth has the same spirit and consciousness as humans. Every aspect of consciousness in the natural world serves as a gateway to pure positive Source energy.

Whether it's plants, flowers, trees, rocks, rivers, the sea, or the wind, they all possess spirit, energy, consciousness, and beingness, just like we do. "Elementals" is a collective term for the spirits and entities of nature.

The elementals are categorized into four main groups:

▷ **Earth elementals** oversee our interactions with the physical world, encompassing aspects such as finances, homes, bodies, and feelings of safety and protection. They are excellent allies in manifesting financial prosperity and fostering a grounded connection to our human existence on this planet. Commonly known as gnomes or faeries, the earth elementals include gnomes, elves, tree dryads, forest nymphs, flower fairies, earth dragons, and mountain giants.

▷ **Air elementals** hold sway over our thoughts and beliefs, including those related to past lives. They support us in releasing limiting thoughts and beliefs, allowing divine guidance to flow freely. Working in conjunction with fire elementals, they aid in reducing stress and finding inner peace. The collective term for air elementals is sylphs, which includes the phoenix, the four winds of the North, South, East, and West, air dragons, and the breeze spirits of desert, mountain, valley, and the ocean.

▷ **Water elementals** are responsible for our sexuality, emotions, and relationships. They embody the Divine Feminine and guide us through our emotional landscape. Skilled relationship experts, they teach us how to handle suppressed emotions, share vulnerably, and cultivate meaningful connections. Collectively referred to as undines, water elementals encompass ocean, lake, and river mermaids, selkies, kelpies, water dragons, water nymphs, and sprites.

▷ **Fire elementals** govern the realms of change, manifestation, motivation, transmutation, and transformation. Representing the Divine Masculine, they instil in us the courage to pursue our aspirations and life purpose. Salamanders, the collective term for fire elementals, include powerful beings such as the phoenix, earth core and volcano dragons, as well as the sunrise, midday, and sunset dragons.

This is not an exhaustive list of elemental beings, but rather a list of the most popular elementals that work with humans for manifestation. You may have noticed that the phoenix is both a fire and an air elemental. This is because it's a blended or composite elemental, made up of both elements. As well as the phoenix, there are many other composite elementals you may connect with. Rather than limiting yourself by only sticking to the ones listed above, let go of your expectations and notice what shows up.

Spiritual Beings

With regards to spiritual beings, you may encounter angels and archangels, Ascended Teachers and Masters, ancestors, star beings, gods and goddesses, and past life soulmates, among others. Again, don't limit yourself by only seeking connection with the aforementioned, but instead be open to seeing who shows up.

When the elemental and spiritual beings do show up, you'll get a sense of them via your five senses. Depending on your main way of receiving intuitive guidance, you may see, feel, or hear them, or just know you're in their presence. Connecting and communicating with the spirit world is a whole different subject, and one that requires more reading and training. To get started, read my book *Secrets of Greek Mysticism* and join my online programme Intuition Mastery School® at www.IntuitionMasterySchool.com.

As you become aware of the beings making contact with you, take some time to get to know them, understand their purpose, and notice what desires they're here to support you with, and how.

Step 4—Receive Energy and Guidance from Your Guides

Having acquainted yourself with the spirit guides that showed up to support you, invite them to charge the energies of your desires with frequencies and guidance that will support their manifestation.

To do so, extend energetic cords from your desires to connect with the spirit guides, and let the guide charge them up with their energy and guidance. While this transmission takes place, you may get ideas and downloads about specific action steps you can take to manifest your desires. Keep an eye out for them and be sure to note them in your journal.

Your spirit guides may also wish to perform a cleansing, healing, or other spiritual ceremony with you. Remember, these spirit guides have already mastered manifestation and have in their arsenal processes and techniques that we can't yet understand. Therefore, be open to their guidance and let them work their magic on you.

When the transmission of guidance feels complete, thank your guides for their support and ask them to stay with you until your desires are fully manifested. Gradually bring some movement into your body and come out of the meditation.

A Note on Spirit Guides

The spirit world is a reflection of the physical world, and so you may encounter spirits that have or don't have your best interests at heart. For this reason, it's important to have sufficient training and discernment before opening yourself up to spiritual beings. To learn how to protect yourself from negative spirit attachments and attack, read my book *Protect Your Light*.

For the purpose of this process, here are some essential guidelines that you can use to differentiate between benevolent and malevolent spirit guides:

▷ Connecting with benevolent spirit guides should always feel positive, loving, and expansive.

▷ Spirit guides should never ask you to harm yourself or someone else.

▷ Spirit guides should never *demand* that you do something. They understand that you have free will, and they'll only advise you.

If any spirit guide acts outside these guidelines, immediately sever the cord you established with them by running your physical hand through the cord. Afterwards, proceed by centring and grounding yourself to regain full control of your energetic presence and power.

From Partying to Purpose

I have countless stories, both personal and client ones, about how our spirit guides can support us in following our purpose and manifesting our desires. However, the one that always pops up when I think about this topic is the following:

During my second year of university, being away from home in a foreign country and on my own, I found myself drawn into the typical student partying culture. It became a weekly routine for me to indulge in excessive drinking and clubbing on Saturday nights.

Each week, I would wake up feeling guilty about my actions, promising myself that I'd never repeat the behaviour. Yet I consistently broke those promises, disregarding the signs that Spirit was sending my way. These signs were clear and persistent: "Quit drinking and commit to your spiritual practice!" Regrettably, I chose to ignore them—until a dramatic event pushed me to reconsider my actions.

One fateful evening, as I prepared for another night of partying, I accidentally stepped on a hot hair-straightening iron left on the floor by my cousin, who had come to visit for the weekend. The burn was severe, leaving a massive blister on my foot, and I was confined to bed for a whole week. When I attempted to pop the blister prematurely, it led to an infection that caused me to limp for an entire month.

This painful experience became a wake-up call, and I finally heeded the signs from the Universe. It was a turning point for me, and I made a firm decision to stop drinking altogether. That night marked the last time I got drunk on a Saturday, and it was years before I even considered taking another sip of alcohol.

While I hadn't consciously connected my desires and purpose to my spirit guides at that time, I had made a dedicated commitment to follow my purpose and asked for their help daily. As a result, my guides began sending me progressively bigger signs, attempting to capture my attention and guide me onto the correct path. Eventually, the signs became so big that I had no choice but to listen.

Today, due to a more conscious and daily practice of cording my desires to specific spirit guides, I am now able to receive moment-to-moment guidance on the actions I need to take to manifest my desires. Moreover, I am aware that, even if I miss certain signs, my guides will find a way to communicate them to me; and, even if I don't grasp them immediately, they will work behind the scenes to steer me in the right direction.

25

NURTURE THE ENERGY OF YOUR DESIRES DAILY

So far, at the fourth step of the manifestation process, you've planted your desires in your energy field, raised their vibration by connecting them with emotional frequencies, and invited cooperative people and spiritual beings to support their manifestation. The final part of nurturing the energy of your desires is to set up a daily practice and maintain these connections, so they may unfold further.

Although going through the previous processes once is sufficient to get the energetic support flowing, it's not enough to sustain it. Energy shifts and changes constantly, from one form to another, so if you don't keep these energetic connections and transmissions active they'll eventually fade away. Therefore, it's important to spend a few minutes daily tuning in and re-energizing the energy attachments you've set up.

The easiest way to accomplish this is to nurture the energy of your desires as part of your daily happiness practice. If you meditate as part of your happiness practice, you can take five to ten minutes of your meditation to consciously become aware of and tend to the energy of your desires and their associated cords.

To do so, go through each desire within your energy field, identify the energetic cords it's connected to, and use your intention to keep the energetic transmission or exchange of energy going.

Cleansing and Shielding Your Desires

As part of nurturing the energy of your desires, it's also important to keep you and your desires cleansed from external, negative, energetic attachments. Therefore it is advisable to work with a daily energy protection practice to maintain your energetic authenticity. Energy protection is the art of being energetically authentic. It's about ensuring that what's yours is yours and what's theirs is theirs. It's about maintaining your alignment with your authentic self and purpose so that your thoughts, emotions, behaviour, and desires are truly yours. Unless you cleanse and protect your energy daily, your energy can be contaminated with other people's energy, and you may end up thinking other people's thoughts, feeling other people's emotions, and behaving in ways that aren't in alignment with your higher self and purpose.

Therefore, by daily cleansing and protecting your energy, you secure the purity and authenticity of your desires, and ensure that the cords you've created are not contaminated or influenced by other people, entities, and energies.

While energy protection goes beyond the scope and purpose of this book, I recommend using the following two practices daily to cleanse and shield your energy and keep the energy of your desires pure and protected. Ideally, practise the following energy protection practices in the morning and as part of your meditation practice, making sure to start with the meditation prep process:

1. **Transmute Negative Energy with the Violet Flame:** The violet flame possesses a high-vibrational frequency capable of transforming negative energy attachments into love and light. It operates at an immensely high frequency, which allows it to transmute all types of energy attack and negativity. Though it shares the violet

colour of the rainbow, its energy is entirely unique, which is why it is often referred to as a flame rather than simply light.

When you're ready to cleanse yourself using the violet flame, simply say, "I summon the violet flame to be with me in this moment. Thank you for flowing through my being, transmuting all negativity, and safeguarding my energy throughout the day." You'll then notice the violet flame surrounding you. Picture it covering your whole body, energy field, and desires, clearing away all low-vibrational energy.

Once your energy and desires feel cleansed, give thanks to the violet flame and proceed with shielding yourself with the rainbow ray.

2. **Raise Your Vibration with the Rainbow Ray**: The rainbow ray consists of the purest and highest-vibrational frequencies of light, incorporating all the colours of your chakras. It has the ability to elevate your energy and enhance your natural defences so that you become invulnerable to energetic attack.

Thus, while the violet flame cleansed your energy by transmuting negative energy attachments into positive energy, the rainbow ray will raise your vibration and the vibration of your desires so that you're protected from attracting negative energy attachments throughout the day.

When you're ready to shield yourself with the rainbow ray, simply say, "I summon the rainbow ray to saturate my energy field and desires, raise my vibration, and protect me from all incoming negative energy throughout the day." Then visualize the rainbow ray manifesting within and around you and enveloping you in a high-vibrational cocoon of rainbow light. With your intention, programme this shield to stay within and around you throughout the day.

Alex's Journey from Personal Assistant to Potter

Alex was a determined personal assistant with a passion for pottery and a dream of starting his own creative business. Fuelled by a burning desire to break free from the confines of his full-time job and embrace his artistic side, he turned to me for guidance on manifesting his purpose.

Following the AMS process, Alex planted the seeds of his purpose and associated desires within his energy field, connecting them with emotional frequencies to raise their vibration. With my guidance, he activated and nurtured these desires daily, inviting supportive energies to aid him in his journey.

The process worked, and as Alex's dedication to his pottery business grew, so did the opportunities to make and sell his ceramic creations. However, just when these opportunities seemed on the verge of materializing, they would unexpectedly fall through, leaving Alex disheartened and perplexed.

Through our work together, we began to understand that the energetic orbs of his desires were tainted by the doubts and fears of those closest to him. Friends and family, with good intentions but limited perspectives, warned him about the risks of leaving his secure job for a creative endeavour. Their limiting beliefs unknowingly influenced the manifestation of his dreams.

I introduced Alex to a daily energy protection practice, during which he learned to cleanse and shield his energy and the energy of his desires from the negative impact of others' opinions. This practice successfully allowed him to release the external limiting beliefs and embrace his purpose fearlessly.

As the months passed, Alex's transformation was remarkable. His pottery business began to flourish, and he started attracting more and more opportunities to showcase and sell his ceramic products. The persistent challenges that had previously hindered his progress vanished, making way for a smooth and unstoppable journey towards his purpose.

In 2023, Alex reached a pivotal moment in his life. The day arrived when he confidently bade farewell to his full-time job as a personal assistant and officially launched his online pottery business. Now, Alex's days are filled with joy and fulfilment, as he spends his time doing what he loves most—creating beautiful pottery that brings smiles to people's faces. The challenges he once faced have been replaced with endless possibilities, and the success of his business continues to grow.

This chapter brings us to the end of the fourth step of the manifestation process. Now you have learned how to nurture the energy of your desires, the final step in the process is to take guided action that will bring your desires to life.

STEP 5

Take Inspired Action

26

TAKE INSPIRED ACTION

So far in the manifestation process, you've raised your vibration, clarified your desires, released the limiting beliefs that prevent you from manifesting them, and nurtured their energy by planting them within your energy field and inviting frequencies, people, and entities to support their manifestation. The final step of the process involves leveraging the previous four steps to receive specific action steps that will allow your desires to come to fruition.

As I explained in Chapter 8, people usually take one of two contrasting approaches when it comes to manifesting their desires. Some people don't have any faith in the Universe to support their manifestation journey, and instead abuse masculine energy by hustling and overworking themselves. On the other hand, others over-depend on the Universe's support and take a passive role in the manifestation process, thus abusing feminine energy and expecting the Universe to do all the work for them.

According to the law of gender, successful, effortless manifestation only takes place when masculine and feminine energies are used together and in a balanced way. Feminine energy allows us to receive inspired guidance as to the specific steps we have to take, and masculine energy plans, orchestrates, and executes that guidance.

We can see how the balance of masculine and feminine energies works together in the manifestation process by observing the cycles of nature. During the winter months, nature is in a primarily feminine state. The trees' leaves fall, vegetation decays, and many animals retreat or hibernate. During this time, nature rests, recalibrates its energies, and receives. In the spring and the summer months, nature shifts into a primarily masculine energy, during which it uses the resources it's nurtured previously to create new life.

Taking guided action towards your desires has to do with emulating this balanced manifestation of masculine and feminine energy, in your day-to-day life. This will allow you to receive the right guidance that will help manifest your desires, and execute that guidance by taking real, palpable steps towards bringing your desires to life.

When it comes to activating masculine and feminine energy, I'm a firm believer in doing so by making real, felt changes in our lives. Although there are many spiritual and energetic meditations you can use to activate these energies, in my experience most people use these meditations to spiritually bypass and avoid doing the real work. Therefore, instead of guiding you through meditation journeys to activating masculine and feminine energy, I'll instead give you practical tips on living a life in which the two energies are balanced.

You can learn even more practices for balancing your masculine and feminine energies for the purpose of manifesting your desires in my book *Lightworkers Gotta Work*. In this book, I guide you to find and define your life purpose, and then share practices for manifesting it by activating and utilizing your balanced masculine and feminine energies.

Linda's Journey to Balancing Masculine and Feminine Energy in Real Estate

Linda was a talented real estate agent from Los Angeles who, after moving to Santa Barbara, experienced a significant dip in her career trajectory. Frustrated and disappointed, she sought guidance and support to regain her momentum and manifest her desires in the real estate market.

Upon our first meeting, I noticed that Linda was well versed in popular manifestation practices such as vision boards, scripting, and positive affirmations. She had also diligently planted her desires into her energy field and nurtured them daily, hoping the Universe would work its magic and bring her the opportunities she sought. However, despite her dedication to these practices, Linda wasn't seeing the results she desired.

Upon deeper exploration, I realized that Linda wasn't lacking opportunities; she was simply not taking practical action towards them. She had become so engrossed in the idea of an ultra-feminine approach to manifestation, where she believed that simply sitting back and receiving would lead to success, that she neglected the essential aspect of taking action.

Together, we dived into the root of her struggles. Linda had developed a fear that taking action would interfere with the mani-festation process, thinking that it would be a sign of pushing against her desires, rather than allowing them to manifest. This mindset was holding her back from reaching her full potential.

Our journey began with me guiding Linda to incorporate daily, physical action steps into her manifestation routine. She needed to call her leads, follow up on potential properties, and be proactive in making things happen.

This transition was challenging for her at first, as it was a signif-icant shift from her previous mindset, but she eventually embraced the change.

I encouraged Linda to see this new approach as a way of co-creating with the Universe, rather than opposing it. By combining the power of her manifestation practices with practical action, she was actively participating in the manifestation process, amplifying the chances of achieving her goals.

With each passing day, Linda grew more confident in her ability to balance her energies and manifest her desires. She took charge of her career, knowing that she was not only attracting opportunities but also making them a reality through her actions.

Soon enough, her efforts started bearing fruit. Linda secured listings and connected with potential clients on a deeper level, thanks to her newfound balanced approach. She no longer feared masculine energy or believed that taking action would hinder her manifestations. Instead, she embraced the harmony of her masculine and feminine energies, recognizing that both were essential for achieving her dreams.

Her reputation as a diligent and proactive real estate agent spread like wildfire, and she quickly reclaimed her position as one of the top agents in Santa Barbara. Linda's success story became an inspiration for others in the industry who were also seeking to find a balance between manifestation and practical action.

As Linda continued to grow, she shared her journey with her colleagues and friends, encouraging them to incorporate both masculine and feminine energies into their manifestation practices. She became an advocate for a balanced approach, emphasizing the importance of actively pursuing one's desires while remaining open to receiving the guidance that the Universe has to offer.

27

ACTIVATE YOUR FEMININE ENERGY

Activating your feminine energy for the purpose of manifestation involves creating time and space to let your mind, body, and spirit receive inspired guidance that will allow you to manifest your desires. Essentially, these receptive practices help you align to Source and your inner being, which is what your daily happiness practice is all about.

Although you're already consciously activating feminine energy through your happiness practice, 30 minutes or an hour of feminine energy at the start of your day isn't enough to balance your masculine and feminine energies. This is especially true if you dedicate the rest of your day to hustling and taking mindless, uninspired action steps, thus abusing your masculine energy.

Conversely, you need equal amounts of feminine and masculine energy time in your days, weeks, months, and year, to optimize your capacity to receive and take inspired action towards the manifestation of your desires.

To help you distinguish between activities related to feminine and masculine energy, in this and the following chapters I'll explain the main characteristics of both energies and share examples of activities related to them. Then, I'll share with you a practical process for balancing these energies in your life.

Feminine Energy Characteristics

Feminine-energy activities tend to have one or more of the following characteristics:

Unstructured

Feminine-energy activities aren't overly planned, directed, or structured. They're activities during which your mind, body, and spirit are free to be, think, and feel freely and without an agenda. Although you can plan to do an unstructured activity, once you're in it there's no or little direction to it.

Examples of unstructured feminine-energy activities involve going out for walks without a destination in mind, going on a spontaneous trip with friends or loved ones, visiting cities and other places without overly planning your activities, or simply sipping on a warm cup of coffee without your phone, TV, or a book to distract you; instead, just spending time with yourself and letting your mind wander.

Restful

Feminine-energy activities allow our mind and body to rest and recalibrate. In a world that glorifies hustle and busyness, we're conditioned to always keep our minds and bodies active. We're constantly thinking about things, chatting with people, and moving from one place to the other, with no time to rest and recalibrate our energy. How can a busy mind and an exhausted body have space to receive divine guidance?

Examples of restful feminine-energy activities involve meditating, sleeping, getting a massage or other spa treatments, and doing any other activity that allows your mind and body to be idle and at peace. Other feminine activities purposely keep your body active to let your mind take a back seat, such as most forms of exercise; usually, when we engage in physical exercise such as walking, swimming, doing yoga, or even working out at the gym, we put most of our focus on our bodies and so give our mind permission to rest.

Reflective

Feminine-energy activities also involve reflecting, processing, and going within. As opposed to the act of thinking, which tends to be more directed and contextual in nature, the act of reflecting asks us to go within with the purpose of understanding and processing our own thoughts, beliefs, and emotional states, as well as other people and the world at large.

For example, doing the inner work to alchemize your fears and limiting beliefs is a feminine-energy activity, as it allows you to reflect, process, and transform your negative emotional states into more positive ones. Other examples of reflective feminine-energy activities involve journaling, pondering, and most self-help processes and modalities that help you shift your thoughts and emotions.

Creative

A misconception about feminine-energy activities is that they're passive, but this couldn't be further from the truth. As *The Kybalion* teaches, feminine energy is the womb that generates our desires and brings them to life. For example, during winter, nature seems idle and passive on the outside, but on the inside it's actively generating new resources in preparation for spring.

Creative activities such as drawing or painting, singing, dancing, and playing musical instruments are examples of things that help us emulate the creative and generative qualities of feminine energy. Creative activities invite us to break free from plans, structures, and stereotypes, and tune in to our innate creativity. As a result, creativity demands that we drop our agenda and allow ourselves to receive guidance from Source. While being creative we let our body and being be an instrument of Source, a womb that creates something totally new.

Surrendering

An important characteristic of feminine energy has to do with letting go and surrendering expectations for results. This is especially true with manifestation, as we often consciously practise manifestation processes with an expectation for an outcome.

The easiest way I've found to surrender my expectation for results is to be aware of the fact that my vibrational frequency isn't the sole cause of my desired effect. Looking back at Chapter 7 and the law of cause and effect, we can see that there are many causes involved in the manifestation process. Following the five-step process explained in this book, or any other processes you choose to use on your manifestation journey, is really all you have control over.

What you don't have control over is the collective vibration, the soul contracts set in place, and the Universe's wisdom as to the right timing for your manifestations to come about. When you accept that it's not totally up to you when and how your desires will manifest, you can surrender your control and trust that it'll all work out eventually.

There are many practices that help you find this state of surrender; these include meditation, prayer, spending time out in nature, and most of the feminine-energy activities mentioned previously.

The common denominator of these five characteristics is their ability to nurture a state of receptivity, which is what feminine energy is truly about. By engaging in activities that are unstructured, restful, reflective, creative, and surrendering, we create energetic space within our mind, body, and spirit, so that they can receive guidance from Source.

How I Awakened My Divine Feminine Energy

Throughout most of my twenties, I found myself immersed in a world of action, hustle, and constant striving. I used to look down on those gentler feminine-energy activities such as resting, surrendering, and reflecting. In my mind, manifesting my dreams and desires required relentless effort and never-ending action.

By my mid-twenties, I had achieved academic success, graduating with bachelor's and master's degrees from prestigious universities in the UK. Living in London and working for a renowned mind, body, spirit publisher, my life seemed on the right track.

Yet beneath the surface I was running on empty. My daily routine was a gruelling cycle of waking up, working, hustling on my own spiritual business, and repeating the same pattern. I had isolated myself from friends and romantic pursuits, believing that success demanded sacrifices. My determination to achieve my dreams at any cost left me physically and mentally drained.

Then, one morning, my body rebelled against this relentless pace. I woke up with the intention of going to work, but my muscles refused to cooperate; I was physically fatigued to the point of my body feeling paralyzed. It was a turning point, forcing me to confront the toll my unbalanced work life had taken on my well-being.

This awakening led me on a transformational journey of self-discovery and conscious growth. I learned to let go of the belief that success had to be achieved through constant struggle. I discovered that manifesting my desires required not just action but also creating space to receive inspired guidance from Source.

I began incorporating feminine-energy practices into my daily routine, allowing myself to rest, reflect, and engage in creative activities without judgement. I learned the art of surrender, releasing my need to control every outcome and trusting in the Universe's timing.

28

PROCESS TO RECEIVE INSPIRED GUIDANCE

The aim of engaging in feminine-energy activities is to receive inspired guidance as to the specific action steps you need to take to manifest your desires and purpose. In this chapter, I'll share with you a process to consciously utilize the aforementioned examples of feminine-energy activities, to successfully receive inspired guidance.

How to Receive Inspired Guidance

Inspired guidance usually pops up as thoughts, ideas, feelings, visions, sounds, and impulses, while engaging in feminine-energy activities. We all receive intuitive messages through all of our five senses, but we usually have one or two senses that are more activated. These are famously known as the four *clairs* or intuition types: clairvoyance, clairsentience, clairaudience, and claircognizance.

The word inspiration comes from the Latin words *in* and *spirare*, and literally means to allow spirit to flow in you, to communicate something. *Inspiration* is closely connected to feminine-energy activities, because to become inspired you have to create mental, emotional, and energetic space to allow for spirit to come in. Feminine-energy activities invite you to clear your mind, relax your body, and free your spirit, thus creating energetic emptiness that can be filled by spirit.

Think back to a time when an epiphany or inspiration hit you. Where were you, and what were you doing? Chances are you were involved in a feminine-energy activity. You may have been out on a hike, practising yoga, meditating, or simply showering (I get most of my ideas and epiphanies in the shower!).

Next, consider how that epiphany came to you. It may have been a thought that just popped in your head (claircognizance), a strong feeling or sensation about something (clairsentience), a vision about you doing something (clairvoyance), or even the voice of something or someone guiding you to do something (clairaudience). Whatever the occasion, that was the Universe communicating with you, and giving you inspired guidance to help you manifest your desires and purpose.

The Difference between Ego and Inspired Guidance

The number one question I get asked when it comes to receiving intuitive and therefore inspired guidance is how to tell whether the guidance comes from our connection to Source, or from our ego.

Here's how to tell the difference between the two:

▷ **Inspired guidance comes first, while the ego's guidance comes next, to sabotage the intuitive message.** This has to do with the nature of the ego; it will almost always doubt an intuitive message in an effort to keep us safe and in our comfort zone. Therefore, it's important to be aware of the ideas and messages that pop up while engaging in feminine-energy activities, and note their timing.

▷ **Inspired guidance feels expansive, while the ego's guidance feels contractive.** When inspired guidance comes in, your body and being agree with it. You feel joy, excitement, and anticipation, and there's a sensation of your energy expanding outwards. Conversely, when it's ego guidance you'll likely feel a contraction within your stomach, associated with low-level emotions such as fear, worry, and apprehension.

▷ **Inspired guidance feels certain, while the ego's guidance feels doubtful.** When you receive inspired guidance, you know it! You don't doubt it and you don't have to ask other people's opinions about it. It feels certain, and therefore you take action towards it. On the other hand, if the guidance you receive comes from the ego you'll likely doubt it and have to get a second opinion about it. I always say, if it's inspired guidance you've already followed it.

Receiving Inspired Guidance Using Automatic Writing

While most of the inspired guidance you receive on your journey will likely be via spontaneous insights while practising a feminine-energy activity, you may also want to take a more direct approach with it.

Automatic writing involves posing a question and allowing Source to intuitively provide the answer through words or drawings. During this process, you open yourself to the flow of the Universe's energy, letting it merge with your consciousness to convey a message. The answers you receive come as intuitive impressions, tailored to your dominant intuition types.

Unlike spiritual possession, where a spirit takes control, automatic writing grants you full awareness and control over yourself. You are responsible for translating the guidance into written form. The mental and energetic state of asking a question differs from receiving the answer, and automatic writing helps you switch between the two effortlessly.

To practise automatic writing, follow these steps:

1. **Frame Your Question:** Rather than binary questions, it's best to ask general and open-ended questions. Ideally, stick to one question at a time, for more focused guidance. Write down your question on paper, as a note on your phone, or as a document on your computer. For manifestation a great question to ask is, "What steps do I need to take to manifest my desire?"

2. **Get into a Meditative State**: Start with the Meditation Prep Process followed by the meditation in Chapter 14, to enter a deep state of meditation. This raises your vibration to connect better with the Universe for effective communication.

3. **Shield Your Energy**: This step protects your energy from unwanted influences. You can use the energy shielding practice in Chapter 25, another shield from my book *Protect Your Light*, or any other energy shield you prefer.

4. **Ask Source to Take Over**: Invite Source, a god or goddess, or another spirit guide you work with to merge with your energy and provide guidance. Visualize golden light entering through your crown chakra and saturating your body and energy.

5. **Automatically Write**: With a relaxed mind and body, open your eyes, take a pen or device, and start answering your written question. The key is to write continuously for at least five minutes without pausing to consider what you're writing. All thoughts, senses, and occurrences from the moment you begin writing are considered intuitive guidance.

As you write, while it is good to be aware of all your *clairs*, pay particular attention to guidance coming through your dominant ones. For example, if you are clairvoyant be mindful of visions in your mind or visual signs in your environment. Focusing on your dominant *clairs*, especially in the beginning, creates a more comfortable and effortless flow of intuitive guidance.

James's Journey of Unlocking His Intuitive Potential

James enrolled in my online course, *Intuition Mastery School*®, with a strong desire to strengthen his intuition. However, he faced a significant challenge—he doubted himself and his intuitive insights, so relied heavily on divination tools like tarot and oracle cards for guidance, using them as a crutch for validation. Deep down, James yearned for a stronger, effortless connection with his intuition.

During our work together, James discovered the practice of automatic writing. Intrigued by its potential, he eagerly embraced it. Nevertheless, like many others he struggled with the common tendency to try to control the process, thus hindering its natural flow.

Guided by the course, James embarked on a journey of healing and self-discovery. He realized that his control issues stemmed from childhood experiences, where he had learned to prioritize people-pleasing and managing others' emotions to gain love and acceptance. His fear of losing control became entangled with feelings of rejection and unworthiness. Only by courageously confronting and healing these deep-seated issues could James find the freedom to relax and let Source take over through automatic writing.

I share James's story to encourage you not to lose hope if your initial attempts at automatic writing don't yield the desired results. Healing past traumas and limiting beliefs opens the door to receiving intuitive guidance and progressing on both the manifestation and intuitive journeys. These paths are interconnected, and the groundwork laid through healing practices is essential for growth.

As James continued to heal and diligently practised automatic writing, he finally liberated himself from his co-dependency on oracle cards and wholeheartedly embraced his inherent ability to receive inspired guidance without relying on external tools.

29

ACTIVATE YOUR MASCULINE ENERGY

Activating your masculine energy for the purpose of manifestation has to do with actualizing the guidance you receive during your feminine-energy activities, to manifest your desires and create real, palpable change in your life and in the world. As discussed previously, we're conditioned to abuse masculine energy by ignoring our intuition and taking mindless action towards our desires and purpose. As a result, our manifestation journey is marked by struggle, overwhelm, and exhaustion.

By understanding the characteristics of healthy masculine energy, you'll be able to balance it with your activated feminine energy and successfully manifest your desires.

Masculine Energy Characteristics

Masculine-energy activities tend to have one or more of the following characteristics:

Structured

Masculine-energy activities are logically structured to take you from point A to point B. They're about taking the abstract ideas and insights you've received during feminine-energy activities, making sense of them, organizing them in your head, and creating a master plan for executing them.

Examples of structured masculine-energy activities include exercises like mind-mapping, planning your week, month, and year using planners and calendars, making to-do lists, researching, and learning skills relevant to your desires and purpose.

Discipline and Consistency

Two essential characteristics of masculine-energy activities are discipline and consistency, which go hand-in-hand. Discipline has to do with sticking to your plans and taking action towards executing them. It's about overcoming procrastination, and being determined and committed enough to focus on the tasks at hand and see them to the finish line. Consistency is about setting daily habits and routines around your goals and plans, so you can gradually complete them.

Examples of such activities include using calendars, planners, and project management applications, setting up systems, and being part of mastermind groups with like-minded people that can keep you accountable. Furthermore, having daily routines is a great way to practise discipline and consistency, as they keep you moving forward without creating overwhelm. For example, I have a daily morning routine around writing my books. Rather than locking myself in the house and writing non-stop, which would make me overwhelmed, I instead write a few pages every day. Therefore, through my writing routine I've disciplined myself to take consistent action towards my desire.

Action-Oriented

Perhaps the most obvious characteristic of masculine-energy activities is that they're action-oriented; about taking forward action towards implementing the plans set in place, and effectively turning ideas into physical creations. These action-oriented activities are usually mental or physical in nature, thus moving you closer to the manifestation of your desires.

Almost all masculine-energy activities are action-oriented in nature, and the actions depend on the plan or desire you're working towards. For example, if your desire is to start a business, action-oriented activities can range from doing market research to designing or sourcing products, creating content, hiring people, etc.

Risk-Taking

Masculine-energy activities are also about having the courage to get out of your comfort zone and take calculated risks towards your desires. Most of the action plans you create towards manifesting your desires will come with resistance. Your ego hates change because it comes with perceived danger, and it'll do everything possible to prevent you from taking forward action. Instead, your ego will want you to stay put in the known reality you feel comfortable in, which comes at the expense of manifesting your desires.

To fully activate masculine energy, you need to embrace the discomfort of risk-taking. You need to accept that taking steps towards your desires and purpose will feel uncomfortable and, rather than shy away from it, find pleasure in doing so. To do so effectively, it's important to take small and calculated risks first so as you don't shock your ego, and then progressively take more courageous risks forward.

Katia's Journey from Wisdom to Action

When I initially began working with Katia, it was evident that she was a personal development junkie. She read countless self-help books, regularly attended a minimum of three personal development retreats each year, and maintained numerous journals filled with notes, insights, and downloads. Yet, while she possessed a deep passion for learning and accumulating spiritual knowledge, she lacked the courage to apply what she learned and just take concrete action.

When I asked Katia whether she was happy with her life and purpose, her expression shifted. It was as if she knew the ingredients for a fulfilling life but couldn't quite put them together. "I can list the steps to leave my job and start my meditation centre," she confessed, "but somewhere between Monday and Wednesday, it all feels too overwhelming, and I stall."

Katia's story resonates with many of us—a shining start followed by a hesitant pause. She was the embodiment of starting projects with zeal, only to be stopped short by overwhelm and self-sabotage.

It became clear that her obstacles were not the usual fears or limiting beliefs that often hinder people. It was a lack of time management and organizational skills that kept her dreams at bay.

Consequently, in our work together we focused on balancing her feminine and masculine energies. I armed Katia with practical tools—a project management software to brainstorm and organize her projects (I recommend Asana, but there are many other great options available), and a daily planner to keep track of her schedule (I like using the Simplified Daily Planner by Emily Ley).

We also had a little heart-to-heart about Katia's to-do lists, transforming them from daunting checklists into manageable pathways to progress. The journey wasn't all smooth sailing. New habits often feel like breaking-in new shoes—a bit awkward at first—but you find your stride eventually.

Katia's transformation unfolded step by step, goal by goal. As she embraced her new routines, her confidence grew, and the unfinished projects on her list started getting crossed off. Today, the pages of her story have reached an exciting chapter; she's on the brink of leaving her job as an executive assistant and launching her meditation centre.

Now that you understand the differences between, and characteristics of, masculine and feminine energies, in the following chapter I'll teach you a process that you can use to ensure that your life is balanced between the two. Achieving this balance in a felt way in your daily life will allow you to effectively and progressively manifest your desires.

30

BALANCE MASCULINE AND FEMININE ENERGY

Balancing your masculine and feminine energy for the purpose of manifestation has to do with ensuring that you spend a relatively equal amount of time in masculine- and feminine-energy activities. This means that you'll have ample time to both receive guidance and take action towards actualizing it.

Most of us are conditioned to abuse either our masculine or feminine energies. Therefore, we need to create a framework through which we can recondition ourselves to use both in a balanced way. The most effective way I've found to do so is by planning my days, weeks, months, and year.

As someone who primarily abused my masculine energy, I found that the easiest way for me to balance it with feminine energy was actually by using a masculine-energy activity—such as planning—to do so. If you've been the same for most of your life, you'll likely find this activity easy to complete.

If, on the other hand, you've mostly overused your feminine energy, then you'll likely feel resistance towards implementing or even trying this process. I'd like you to see this as your opportunity to take a risk outside of your comfort zone, and activate your masculine energy by going through this process.

Planning Your Life for Balance

In the following sections, I'll share with you tips and guidance to balancing your masculine and feminine energies within the year, its months, weeks, and days.

Plan Your Year

It's best to start this exercise a couple of months before, or right at the start of, the new year. Take out your journal and make a list of large-scale masculine- and feminine-energy activities that you wish to execute in the new year.

Masculine-energy activities will likely be bigger projects and goals that stem from your desires and purpose, such as launching a new product or course, completing a training, or writing a book. Large-scale activities governed by feminine energy will usually be your main vacation times for the year; longer periods of time during which you can do more feminine-energy activities. For example, this might be a Christmas or summer vacation, or any other trips or time off that you wish to take in the following year.

Depending on the nature of your job and how much vacation time you can realistically take, try to ensure that you schedule as many feminine activities as you do masculine ones. For example, if you've decided to work on three large-scale projects in the coming year, then schedule vacation periods in between them, so your year is balanced in masculine and feminine energy.

Once you've finalized your main projects and vacation times for the year, get a yearly wall calendar and roughly block the days or months you plan to work on these.

Plan Your Months

Having blocked out your main projects and vacation times on your yearly calendar, you'll then have a rough outlook of what you need to focus on, month by month.

To ensure you stick to this plan and create further balance during the year, it's a good idea to spend some time before each month begins to plan the month ahead. I like to use a physical planner to do so, but you can use a digital one on your phone or computer if you prefer.

During this time, consult with your master plan to see what projects you need to be focusing on. If there's too much work and not much pleasure ahead, adjust your month's plan by adding new, feminine-energy activities that'll balance things out.

For example, if you have a deadline for the end of the month that you know will require you to work long hours, make sure you schedule extra time off at the weekends or in the evenings, to plan trips or do other feminine-energy activities.

Plan Your Weeks

Every weekend, go through the activities planned for the following week and ensure that your week is balanced in masculine and feminine energy. Check that you have plenty of time scheduled to take action towards your desires and purpose, but that you also have time to rest and recalibrate your energy.

Learning to set boundaries with your time and energy is an important skill to develop, so that you stick to your plan and don't end up abusing either your masculine or feminine energies. For example, my personal boundaries are to work four days a week, finish work at 8 p.m., and then spend the weekend doing feminine-energy activities. Depending on the nature of your work, come up with boundaries that help you uphold your balanced weekly schedule.

Plan Your Days

Finally, at the start of each day take some time to look through your weekly schedule and structure your day so that it's balanced in masculine- and feminine-related activities.

Ensure that you have enough action steps scheduled, which will allow you to move your desires forward, but also have plenty of time to rest and receive inspired guidance.

Being Flexible with Your Plans

Having planned my life this way since 2018, I've learned that, while the process works, it's also important to be flexible with it. If you're someone who has largely abused masculine energy in their life, it'll be easy to become enslaved to this process and let it dictate how you live your life, rather than the other way around. Remember, this process is meant to be a tool that you use consciously to balance your life and manifest your desires. Don't fall into the trap of letting the process have agency over you instead and thus give your power away.

To find this balance, aim to do the best you can to come up with your yearly, monthly, weekly, and daily plans, but then allow these plans to ebb and flow according to what comes up in your life. For example, if you've planned to launch a new course in May, but an event opportunity comes up that you feel excited about, give yourself permission to move things around and do what lights you up.

When we plan things in advance, we often do so by thinking logically and in terms of time and space, but we don't and can't possibly take into consideration how we'll feel at the time, personal circumstances, world events, or anything else that may come up. Thus, while I'm a huge supporter of planning, I also understand that plans can and should change when new and better opportunities arise.

I'm sure you've heard of the Yiddish proverb, "We plan, God laughs." While many people use this proverb to justify not planning anything and just taking things as they come, I personally see it as guiding us to be flexible with our planning instead. The proverb reminds us of the many different "causes" that may be working behind the scenes but which we're not familiar with, as we've explored in the chapter on the law of cause and effect. Thus, we plan our lives based on the factors and causes we have control over, but also know that the Universe is aware of additional factors that we may not know of or have any control over.

If the idea of planning the entire year in advance feels too overwhelming and you seek even more flexibility, then I'd suggest either planning things quarterly or biannually. This way, you get to have a better idea of what's ahead so you can plan your time more accurately.

Planning your life in this way may initially feel like a masculine-oriented way to live, but it's really a balanced approach, because you're planning an equal amount of masculine and feminine activities. This process ensures that you don't simply experience energetic balance once in a while when you do a meditation, but instead experience that balance every single day of your life. Most importantly, this process ensures that you're not a passive viewer in the manifestation of your desires, but instead are a cooperative component who's collaborating with the Universe to bring your desires and purpose to life.

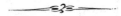

3

10-DAY
MANIFESTATION
CHALLENGE

So far in our journey together, you've learned about the seven laws of the Universe and have equipped yourself with a five-step process to put them into practice. In this final part of the book, I invite you to join me on a ten-day manifestation challenge to manifest a specific desire!

Every day, I'll give you an actionable step that draws from what you've learned so far and builds on the previous one, to help you manifest your chosen desire. The steps will be easy to complete and won't take you more than 15 minutes daily. All you'll need is your journal to complete the daily practices, your meditation space, and trust in yourself and the process.

Challenges work best when you have someone keeping you accountable, so feel free to invite a friend to join you. Alternatively, you can share a picture of you completing each day in the **Your Spiritual Toolkit** Facebook group, or on Instagram, by tagging **@georgelizos** and using the hashtag **#AMSChallenge**.

Day 1

CHOOSE YOUR DESIRE

Welcome to the first day of the challenge!

Before you clarify the desire you want to manifest, it's important to first take time to raise your vibration. If you've been applying the processes taught in the book so far, you have raised your vibration sufficiently and may already have specific desires in mind. If you haven't applied the processes yet, be sure to at least complete the processes in Chapter 22, Raise the Vibration of Your Desires, before you get started with the challenge.

Not every desire can be manifested in ten days. Remember, that there are many different factors contributing to the manifestation of your desires, so ten days may not be sufficient for you to manifest *any* desire.

Therefore, when it comes to choosing a desire to work on for this challenge, I suggest that you choose a desire that you feel is *possible* to manifest in ten days but probably unlikely. This is a good balance of choosing something relatively easy to manifest, but which will still require collaborative manifestation effort to come to fruition. There's no exact science to choosing the right desire, so just use this rule of thumb and trust your gut! Even if you choose a desire that's not possible to manifest in ten days, you'll still be closer to manifesting it by the end of this challenge. So, you can't really get it wrong.

Complete the Challenge

1. With your life purpose in mind, brainstorm possible desires in your journal. Don't hold back at this stage; simply share every desire that comes to mind.

2. Now, go through the above desires and choose the one that's possible but unlikely to manifest within ten days. Circle that desire in your journal—or better, write it on a Post-it note and place it somewhere you can see it daily.

Day 2

IDENTIFY YOUR FEARS AND LIMITING BELIEFS

What fears and limiting beliefs do you have that prevent you from manifesting your chosen desire? For the second day of the challenge, you'll use the *Five Whys* process in Chapter 16 to dig deep into your fears and limiting beliefs and identify the core beliefs that are blocking you from manifesting your specific desires.

An easy way to identify these fears and limiting beliefs is by asking yourself the following questions:

▷ How do I feel about having this?

▷ Do I deserve this? Why, or why not?

▷ What's preventing me from having this?

Complete the Challenge

1. Use your journal to answer these questions and come up with a list of all the fears and limiting beliefs that prevent you from having your chosen desire.

2. Choose one or a few of the statements that feel most dominant, and use the *Five Whys* process to identify the core beliefs behind them.

3. Once you've identified the core beliefs, circle or write them down clearly so you can release them in the next couple of days.

Day 3

RELEASE YOUR CORE LIMITING BELIEFS COGNITIVELY

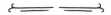

Having identified the core beliefs preventing you from manifesting your chosen desire, it's now time to release them, cognitively and energetically. Today, we'll focus on cognitively releasing them using the IEMT process in Chapter 12. Your core beliefs were created as a result of a series of past experiences. With this process, you'll get to identify these experiences and desensitize them, thus updating your perception of yourself, others, and the world.

Complete the Challenge

1. Take yourself through the IEMT process and briefly write down the memories related to your core beliefs as they come up, so you can more easily remember them while using the eye-movement process.

2. Once you've finished with the process, consider your original core limiting beliefs. To what degree are these beliefs still true for you? If they're still true, repeat the process. If not, share your newfound beliefs in your journal.

Day 4

RELEASE YOUR CORE LIMITING BELIEFS ENERGETICALLY

Having released your core limiting beliefs cognitively using IEMT, you'll now get to release them energetically, too. Use the process in Chapter 13 to do so, and share your insights in your journal by answering the following questions.

Complete the Challenge

1. Where were the core limiting beliefs located in your energy field?
2. How did they look, feel, or sound? Describe them.
3. How did you feel after releasing them? Did any insights come to mind?

Remember, after releasing limiting beliefs energetically you may go through a period of mental, emotional, and physical purging. To support yourself through this process, make sure to drink plenty of water, eat healthily, and move your body. This will allow the toxins to flush out of your system faster.

Day 5

CREATE NEW, SUPPORTIVE BELIEFS

Congratulations for getting halfway through the challenge! You've already completed the toughest part, so the rest of it will be easy breezy fun.

Today, you'll get to replace the core limiting beliefs you've released in the previous two exercises, with new, supportive beliefs.

Complete the Challenge

1. Use the process in Chapter 20 to create new, positive beliefs, and then write them down in your journal in the form of positive affirmations.

2. To strengthen your connection to these new beliefs, connect energetically to them by completing the process in the chapter.

3. Finally, ensure that you read these affirmations out loud to yourself every day for the rest of this challenge, or for as long as it takes you to manifest your desire. You may want to write them down on a separate piece of paper and stick it somewhere you can see it daily, to remind yourself to do so.

Day 6

PLANT YOUR DESIRE IN YOUR ENERGY FIELD

Having released the limiting beliefs that may hinder you from manifesting your desire and created new supportive ones, you're now ready to start nurturing the energy of your desire so that you can magnetize it to you.

Complete the Challenge

Use the process in Chapter 21 to plant the energy of your desire in your energy field, ensuring that you spend some time matching your frequency to it and feeling the exchange of energy. After you've done so, answer the following questions in your journal:

1. How would you describe the energy of your desire? Share its colour, texture, sound, taste, and any associated thoughts or emotions that come up while connecting with it.
2. How did it feel aligning yourself to the frequency of your desire? Did you notice any changes to your own energy as a result?

Day 7

RAISE THE FREQUENCY OF YOUR DESIRE

Now that your desire is firmly planted within your energy field, you're ready to raise its vibration and speed up the manifestation process.

Complete the Challenge

Using the process in Chapter 22, choose up to three emotional frequencies to connect your desire to. This will raise the vibration of your desire and turn it into a powerful emotional magnet that will attract to you people, circumstances, opportunities, and other cooperative components that aid its manifestation.

Once you're done with the process, answer the following questions in your journal:

1. What emotional frequencies have you chosen to connect your desire to?

2. How did the energy of your desire shift as a result of tuning it to these frequencies? Describe the changes in colour, texture, frequency, sound, taste, etc.

3. Did you receive any insights around specific action steps you can take to help manifest your desire?

Day 8

INVITE HELPFUL PEOPLE TO SUPPORT YOU

Having already nurtured the energy of your desires, both with your supporting new beliefs and connecting your desire to your energy field and other emotional frequencies, you'll likely start seeing manifestation evidence of your desire coming to life.

Before you continue with today's challenge, write down in your journal any manifestation evidence that's come up. This needn't be physical evidence necessarily, but also ideas that came up, signs and synchronicities that you're getting closer, people you meet or observe who already have your desire, etc.

Writing down the manifestations that have come up already is also a great way to keep the momentum going. There are only two days left on this challenge, so let's finish strong!

Complete the Challenge

Today, we'll continue the process of nurturing the energy of your desire by energetically inviting helpful people to support you in manifesting it. To do so, follow the steps of the process in Chapter 23. Once you've done so, answer the following questions in your journal:

1. Out of the many filaments you sent out, how many turned into cords and connected with helpful people?

2. Did you get a sense of who these people might be? Aside from strangers, there will likely be people who're already in your life. List them in your journal, along with any ways through which they may help you to manifest your desire.

Day 9

INVITE SPIRIT GUIDES TO SUPPORT YOU

Today is the final day of nurturing the energy of your desire, this time by inviting spirit guides to support you in manifesting it. Remember, that manifestation is a collaborative process. You take some action, the Universe (including your spirit guides) also takes some action, and together you bring your desire to life.

Complete the Challenge

Go through the process in Chapter 24 to invite spirit guides to support you, and then answer the following questions in your journal:

1. What spirit guides showed up to support your manifestation journey? Share the type of guides, their names if given, and what they're here to help you do specifically.
2. What insights did your spirit guides impart with regards to manifesting your specific desire? You may have received these insights as thoughts, ideas, images, feelings, sounds, or simply energy.

Day 10

CREATE A BALANCED ACTION PLAN

Congratulations! You've made it to the final day of the challenge. Today will be about reaping the fruits of your labour, and keeping the momentum going.

By this stage you may have already manifested your desire. If you have, take a moment to appreciate yourself and the journey, and complete the Manifestation Challenge Review on the next page. If your desire hasn't manifested yet, or has only partly manifested, continue with today's challenge.

Complete the Challenge

So far, the action steps you've taken have been about reprogramming your beliefs and nurturing the energy of your desire. Now comes the more practical side of the process, which involves taking forward action towards bringing your desire to life.

Use the automatic writing process in Chapter 28 to consciously receive your next action steps to manifesting your desire. After completing the process, answer the following questions:

1. What are your next action steps to manifesting your desires? Make an exhaustive list of everything that's come up.

2. Use these action steps to create a balanced plan of action for the next two weeks, to keep the momentum going. Use the guidance in Chapters 27, 29, and 30 to come up with both feminine- and masculine-energy activities that can help you move closer to manifesting your desires.

3. Schedule these activities and action steps in your chosen planner and make sure to follow through.

MANIFESTATION CHALLENGE REVIEW

At the end of the ten days of taking daily, consistent action towards manifesting your desire, it's a good idea to review the process so you can optimize it moving forward.

If you are extending the manifestation challenge by completing the two-week balanced action plan from Day 10, complete this review at the end of the two-week period.

Review your progress by journaling on the following questions:

1. Did you end up manifesting your chosen desire? To what degree have you done so?

2. If you haven't fully manifested your desire, what evidence have you received that you're getting closer to doing so?

3. What obstacles have you faced while going through this challenge? Did any additional fears or limiting beliefs come up?

4. How can you improve and optimize the process moving forward?

Whether you've succeeded in manifesting your chosen desire or not, take the opportunity to congratulate yourself for completing this challenge! You've showed up, done the work, and got results, whatever they may have been. What matters is not the degree to which you've manifested your desire, but you taking action towards doing so. It's only through consistent engagement with the manifestation process that you'll get to optimize it, so that you can progressively improve on and master your manifestation game.

CONCLUSION

Oh my goodness, you've made it to the end of the book! Congratulations! I'm so proud of you, and you should be too. In our journey through this book, you've learned about the seven manifestation laws of the Universe and have encountered a five-step process of putting them into action, and you have equipped yourself with brand-new, cognitive and energetic processes for collaborating with the Universe to manifest your desires.

As our journey together in this book comes to an end, I'd like to emphasize the biggest takeaways of this work. These are the pieces that made the most impact on me while I was rediscovering manifestation, and ultimately helped me master it.

Manifestation Is a Collaborative Process

I hope that the most important message you've taken away from this book is that manifestation is a collaborative process. Although your personal vibrational frequency is the main determining factor to manifesting your desires, there are other factors that contribute to the process, such as soul contracts, your life and soul purposes, collective manifestation, and taking action towards your desires, among others. Simultaneously, rather than the law of attraction or vibration being the only determining law in manifestation, in truth it always works in accordance with the other many laws of the Universe.

When this understanding sinks in, you'll finally let yourself off the hook and start enjoying, rather than resenting, the manifestation process.

I remember a time when I constantly felt guilty and inadequate for not getting manifestation right. I was stuck thinking that I wasn't doing it right, and compared myself to the "manifestation gurus" who claimed they had the answers. What freed my frustration wasn't optimizing what I had already known, but empowering myself with knowledge I previously hadn't had. I hope that learning about the seven laws of the Universe has had the same impact with you, too.

The Universe Will Show Up for You, If *You* Show Up for You

"The possession of knowledge, unless accompanied by a manifestation and expression in action, is like the hoarding of precious metals—a vain and foolish thing. Knowledge, like wealth, is intended for use. The Law of Use is universal, and he who violates it suffers by reason of his conflict with natural forces."
—The Kybalion

This is one of my favourite quotes from *The Kybalion*, and something I've believed and practised for years. When you look at the spiritual community in general, the main focus is on experiencing rather than doing. We're conditioned to believe that experiencing a meditation and going through a healing session equal doing the work. When the change we expect doesn't happen, we think it's because we haven't done something right or enough, and go off and do more energy work. I call this spiritual entertainment.

Instead, I believe in practical spirituality. Don't get me wrong, I'm all about meditation and energy healing journeys. This is, in fact, the main pillar of my work. However, I'm also about doing the real, physical, palpable work that comes after the energy work. Energy and spiritual work are simply the beginning of the healing, spiritual, or manifestation process, not the end. Unless we take real action steps to actualize what we experience energetically, we end up where we first started.

When it comes to manifestation specifically, your desires and purpose won't manifest with you sitting on a meditation pillow all day long. After you're done with your manifestation practice, it's important to get off the meditation pillow and take consistent action steps aimed at bringing your desires to life. If you don't, then you're not being a cooperative component in the manifestation process. All other manifestation factors may be working for you, but your inactivity may be blocking things from manifesting.

Negative Emotions Aren't Negative

Most manifestation books vilify negative emotions and instead foster denial and toxic positivity. Rather than resolving and expressing our negative thoughts, beliefs, and emotions, we're instead guided to suppress them, look the other way, or try to think positively. In truth, none of these practices work.

By suppressing, looking the other way, or distracting yourself with something positive, you only strengthen your negative emotions, thoughts, or beliefs. Yes, you may succeed in feeling better in the short term, but, unless you actually express and resolve the root cause of your negative states, ignoring them will only make them stronger and louder, until they eventually burst out and wreak havoc in your life. In the meantime, the energetic presence of your negative emotions, thoughts, and beliefs in your energy field will keep your vibration low, sabotaging your manifestation practice.

For this reason, I believe that *doing the inner work* should be part of every manifestation process. Rather than lowering your vibration, when done right, feeling and processing your negative states will release or transmute them, and then you'll be truly able to feel better and raise your vibration.

How to Move Forward

There are a few options for moving forward from here. If you've chosen to read the book first before applying the processes, it's time to get your journal out, choose your meditation spot and get started. Download the *Ancient Manifestation Secrets* Cheat Sheet to keep track of your progress; this can be found at **GeorgeLizos.com/AMS.**

If you've been doing the processes and meditations while reading the book, here's your next plan of action:

1. **Revise the seven laws of the Universe:** Although you may have previously been aware of some of the laws, such as the law of vibration and law of polarity, you probably didn't know them all. You've probably been conditioned to think of the law of vibration (attraction) as the holy grail of manifestation; so, the more you familiarize yourself with all seven laws, the easier it'll be for you to put them into practice, and consider them when going about your manifestation practice.

2. **Keep doing the inner work:** Doing the inner work of releasing limiting thoughts, emotions, and beliefs isn't a one-off practice. It's something you will do for the rest of your life. Limiting beliefs are multilayered, in the sense that they may take months, if not years, to be fully released. As you progress with your manifestation journey, it's important to be aware of your triggers, and use them to access and release the layers of your limiting beliefs, as these come up.

3. **Have a daily manifestation practice:** Remember, the Universe will show up for you, if *you* show up for you. To consciously manifest your desires, you need to take consistent action to do so. Sure, you can surrender completely and let things unfold as they will,

but that's not why you picked up this book. You're someone who wants to have an active role in the manifestation process, so make sure you do so. The easiest way to stick to your manifestation practice is to combine it with your daily happiness practice.

Last but not least, take a playful approach to doing this work. Life is meant to be enjoyed, so don't get overly controlling with your manifestation practice. Being in a joyful, high-vibe state is the most important factor to manifestation. Therefore, if you catch yourself feeling less than joyful in your practice, pause and pivot. Revise your practice so that it feels light and enjoyable, and keep doing so moving forward.

———◁⧗▷———

ACKNOWLEDGEMENTS

To Gods Apollo, Hermes, and Athena, thank you for inspiring and writing this book through me. It's an honour to follow your guidance and live your path.

To Emma Mumford, thank you for your friendship, support, and writing the most magical and heartfelt foreword to introduce this book to the world.

Thank you, Gala Darling, Jy Prikulshnik, Amy Leigh Mercree, Sherianna Boyle, Tammy Mastroberte, Elyse Welles, Kelsey Aida, Suzy Ashworth, and Ali Levine, for your generous endorsements and support.

I'm grateful to the entire team at Findhorn Press and Inner Traditions for trusting in me and this book.

Thank you to Lena and Panos at Nefeles Guesthouse in Delphi, Greece, for welcoming me into their home and creating a magical sanctuary for me to write this book.

To you, the reader, thank you for joining me on this journey to learning about manifesting your life and purpose.

ABOUT THE AUTHOR

George Lizos is a spiritual teacher, psychic healer, priest to Hellenic Polytheism, creator of *Intuition Mastery School®* as well as a number one bestselling author (*Be the Guru, Lightworkers Gotta Work, Protect Your Light, Secrets of Greek Mysticism*) and host of *The Lit Up Lightworker* and *Can't Host* podcasts. He helps lightworkers to overcome the fears and limiting beliefs that prevent them from finding and following their life's purpose of finding happiness, helping others to heal, and raising the vibration of the world.

He has been named one of the top 50 health and wellness influencers, and his work has been featured in Goop, MindBodyGreen, POPSUGAR, *Soul & Spirit, Spirit & Destiny, Kindred Spirit*, and Watkin's *Mind Body Spirit*. He holds bachelor's and master's degrees in metaphysical sciences, a BSc. in human geography with focus on sacred geographies, an MSc. in psychology, an MSc. in business management, and a diploma in acting.

George took part in the first official priesthood training in Hellenic polytheism, organized by the Supreme Council of Ethnic Hellenes (YSEE) in Athens, following the religion's legal recognition by the Greek government in 2017. Since then, he's been a practising priest of the religion at the world's first modern temple of Zeus in Cyprus. George has taught about Greek spirituality and manifestation in his books, workshops, and online courses for more than 15 years.

WORK WITH ME

GET WEEKLY TOOLS

Download my FREE *Discover Your Life Purpose* guide to find and define your life purpose in a specific, two-paragraph definition. You'll also receive my weekly newsletter with more tools and guidance. Get it at **www.georgelizos.com/lifepurpose**.

WORK WITH ME

If you've enjoyed this book and want to go deeper with your journey, check out my online courses, meditations, and private sessions at **www.georgelizos.com/work-with-me**.

GET SUPPORT

Meet like-minded lightworkers, learn new spiritual practices, and attend exclusive workshops within my private Facebook group, **Your Spiritual Toolkit, www.yourspiritualtoolkit.com**.

FEEL INSPIRED

My *Lit Up Lightworker* podcast features interviews with leading spiritual teachers on various spiritual topics, while my *Can't Host* podcast provides guidance and education on sex and relationships for gay, queer, and bisexual men. Check them out on Apple Podcasts, Spotify, and all main podcast platforms.

STAY IN TOUCH

Tell me all about your experience with manifesting your desires on **Instagram (@georgelizos)**.

FINDHORN PRESS

Life-Changing Books

Learn more about us and our books at
www.findhornpress.com

For information on the Findhorn Foundation:
www.findhorn.org